T0339476

Brexit and Procurement Law

Public procurement law, regulating public sector purchasing of certain contracts for goods, works and services, is an area of EU law which is closely intertwined with the UK's economy. It will almost inevitably be affected by the consequences of Brexit.

At a time of significant uncertainty, this book explores policy directions which domestic procurement law could take in the future, including whether 'Buy National' policies might feasibly be introduced, or whether existing procurement procedures could be significantly reviewed.

Catherine Maddox is a solicitor practising EU law in London.

Legal Perspectives on Brexit
Series Editor: Richard Lang, University of Brighton, UK
Editorial Board: David Edward CMG, QC, MA, LLB, LLD, FRSE
(University of Edinburgh, UK, *Emeritus*)
Margot Horspool (University of Surrey, UK, *Emeritus*)
Shirley McDonagh (CILEx, UK)

Legal Perspectives on Brexit is a peer-reviewed series of shortform books which goes beyond responding to public curiosity aroused by the triggering of Article 50 to recognize the ongoing legal and political disputes Brexit has prompted. Aimed at academics and professionals, it provides expert commentary on and predictions about the possible legislative and judicial implications of Brexit for each of the different sectors of regulation which have for so long been dominated by EU Law, creating a valuable one stop resource which exposes, explores and perhaps even resolves legal problems stemming from the separation of UK and EU legal systems.

Brexit and Aviation Law
Jan Walulik

Brexit and Intellectual Property Law
Janice Denoncourt

Brexit and Competition Law
Andreas Stephan and Barry Rodger

Brexit and Energy Law
Raphael Heffron

https://www.routledge.com/law/series/BREXIT

Brexit and Procurement Law

Catherine Maddox

LONDON AND NEW YORK

First published 2019
by Routledge
2 Park Square, Milton Park, Abingdon, Oxon OX14 4RN

and by Routledge
605 Third Avenue, New York, NY 10017

First issued in paperback 2021

Routledge is an imprint of the Taylor & Francis Group, an informa business

Publisher's Note
The publisher has gone to great lengths to ensure the quality of this reprint but
points out that some imperfections in the original copies may be apparent.

British Library Cataloguing-in-Publication Data
A catalogue record for this book is available from the British Library

Library of Congress Cataloging-in-Publication Data
Names: Maddox, Catherine, author.
Title: Brexit and procurement law / Catherine Maddox.
Description: Abingdon, Oxon [UK]; New York, NY: Routledge, 2018. |
Series: Legal perspectives on Brexit | Includes bibliographical
references and index.
Identifiers: LCCN 2018044751 | ISBN 9781138591073 (1)
Subjects: LCSH: Government purchasing—Law and legislation—
Great Britain. | Government purchasing—Law and legislation—
European Union countries. | Public contracts—Great Britain. |
Public contracts—European Union countries. |
European Union—Great Britain.
Classification: LCC KD1610 .M33 2018 | DDC 346.4102/3—dc23
LC record available at https://lccn.loc.gov/2018044751

ISBN 13: 978-1-03-224166-1 (pbk)
ISBN 13: 978-1-138-59107-3 (hbk)

DOI: 10.4324/9780429955600

Typeset in Times New Roman
by codeMantra

In memory of Penelope, who could listen to the grass grow and the squirrel's heart beat. With thanks to DRMV, SG, IA, MM and my cousins.

Contents

x   *Contents*

PART II
Key Legislation and Recommended Reading   63

Abbreviations and definitions

Abbreviations

CCR 2016	Concession Contracts Regulations 2016
CETA	Canada's Comprehensive Economic and Trade Agreement with the EU
CJEU	Court of Justice of the European Union
DCFTA	Ukraine's Deep and Comprehensive Free Trade Area with the EU
Directive 2014/23	Directive 2014/23/EU
Directive 2014/24	Directive 2014/24/EU
DWA	European Commission Draft Withdrawal Agreement
EEA	European Economic Area
EFTA	European Free Trade Association
ESPD	European Single Procurement Document
EU 27	European Union 27 Member States
EUWA	European Union (Withdrawal) Act
GATS	General Agreement on Trade in Services
GATT	General Agreement on Tariffs and Trade
GPA	Government Procurement Agreement
PCR 2015	Public Contracts Regulations 2015 (as amended)
WTO	World Trade Organisation

Definitions

Brexit: The British exit from the EU, that is, the UK's departure from the European Union

Exit Day: 11.00 p.m. 29 March 2019

Transition Period: from Exit Day to 31 December 2020

UK or domestic procurement law: procurement law in England and Wales

Introduction

Public procurement law, which regulates[1] public sector purchasing of certain contracts for goods, works and services, will almost inevitably be affected by the consequences of Brexit.[2,3] Domestic procurement legislation may need to be reconsidered and revised to accommodate both the nature of the UK's changing relationship with the European Union and the UK's developing domestic policy goals. At a time of significant uncertainty about an area of EU law which is so closely intertwined with the UK's economy, this book explores the various policy directions which domestic procurement law could take in the future. Examples include whether 'Buy National' policies might feasibly be

---

1 Organisation for Economic Co-operation and Development, 'Government at a Glance' (*OECD Statistics*, 2017) <http://stats.oecd.org/Index.aspx?QueryId=78406> accessed 3 June 2018
2 Throughout this book 'Exit Day' is referred to as the date currently specified as 11.00 p.m. 29 March 2019; at the time of writing, the intention is that the UK will leave the EU on this date, unless the EU and UK agree otherwise. The transition period which is scheduled to follow Exit Day is currently due to end on 31 December 2020. European Union (Withdrawal) Act 2018, S.20 (1)
   The date of Exit Day is two years after the UK gave notification to trigger Article 50. Article 50(3) of the Treaty on European Union states; 'The Treaties shall cease to apply to the State in question from the date of entry into force of the withdrawal agreement or, failing that, two years after the notification referred to in paragraph 2, unless the European Council, in agreement with the Member State concerned, unanimously decides to extend this period'; Consolidated Version of the Treaty on European Union [2012] OJ C 326, Article 50 <https://eur-lex.europa.eu/legal-content/EN/TXT/?uri=CELEX%3A12012M050> accessed 9 June 2018
3 The UK government has proposed that the transition period should have a flexible end date, determined by how long it will take to prepare and implement the new processes and new systems; HM Government, *Response to EU Commission's position paper of 7 February 2018, Article X Implementation Period* (Explanatory Note 2018) <https://assets.bwbx.io/documents/users/iqjWHBFdfxIU/rQVCUXtdp4QM/v0> accessed 10 June 2018

introduced, or whether existing procurement procedures could be significantly reviewed. This book investigates the possible impacts of Brexit on existing procurement legislation (for example, whether key pieces of legislation will be retained or significantly revised) and discusses the future of the legal relationship between UK public procurement legislation and EU public procurement case law.

It may initially seem that the development of procurement law after Brexit is a slightly academic subject, remote from everyday life and only of interest to academics, lawyers and public procurement practitioners. However, public procurement law regulates the use of taxpayers' money in many key areas which impact directly on daily life, from the regeneration of local areas, the construction of schools and hospitals, to the collection of waste and street cleaning. Every taxpayer has an interest in whether the tendering processes for private operators of these services are run equitably and transparently and whether value for money is achieved. Therefore, any proposed changes to the current system merit a high degree of public scrutiny.

How to use this book

The book is divided into two parts. Part I comprises the majority of the book, exploring the challenges and opportunities provided by Brexit. There are four main topic areas in Part I. First, the legal and political context for the future of procurement law. Second, a detailed exploration of the procurement law provisions in the European Commission Draft Withdrawal Agreement. Third, the impact of the loss of access to EU online tools, universal classification systems and other guidance. Fourth, a brief exploration of the potential impact of the reduction of access to procurement markets.

Part II offers an overview of the impact of Brexit on UK procurement law legislation depending on the type of deal agreed when the UK exits the European Union. It summarises what matters in procurement law may stay the same, which minor issues may require attention and which major issues will need urgent resolution. It also offers a bibliography for further reading.

This book can be used by public procurement legal practitioners, students of procurement law and the general reader who has a special interest in the legal basis and development of procurement law after Brexit.

Part I

Challenges and Opportunities

Challenges

1 Legal and political context for the future of procurement law

Current legal framework for UK procurement law

This book focuses on two key EU public procurement directives which have been transposed into UK[1] law.[2]

1 Directive 2014/24/EU ("Directive 2014/24") on the public sector, implemented by the Public Contracts Regulations 2015 (as amended) ("PCR 2015")
2 Directive 2014/23/EU ("Directive 2014/23") on concession contracts, implemented by the Concession Contracts Regulations 2016 ("CCR 2016")

Both of these EU directives are relatively recent. The domestic procurement legislation, the PCR 2015[3] and CCR 2016[4] are to a large extent a copy-out of Directives 2014/24[5] and 2014/23[6]

1 When this book refers to UK or domestic procurement law, it is referring to procurement law in England and Wales.
2 Another Directive, not covered in this book, is Directive 2014/25 on utilities which repealed Directive 2004/17/EC on procurement in the water, energy, transport and postal service sectors. There is also EU legislation in respect of defence procurement, which is not covered in this book.
3 Public Contracts Regulations 2015 (SI 2015/102) (as amended)
4 Concession Contracts Regulations 2016 (SI 2016/273)
5 Directive 2014/24/EU of the European Parliament and of the Council of 26 February 2014 on public procurement and repealing Directive 2004/18/EC Text with EEA relevance, OJ L 94, 28.3.2014, pp. 65–242
6 Directive 2014/23/EU of the European Parliament and of the Council of 26 February 2014 on the award of concession contracts Text with EEA relevance, OJ L 94, 28.3.2014, pp. 1–64

("the Directive(s)"), with some UK-specific amendments and additions.[7]

The Directives were drafted as part of a revision of the previous EU procurement regime. The key principles of EU public procurement did not change during this revision process; contracts were still to be competed and awarded transparently and without discrimination. The revision aimed to simplify procedures and better enable public authorities to use public procurement to achieve public policy goals.

Other amendments were as a result of case law from the Court of Justice of the European Union ("CJEU") and represented the codification of principles which were already being utilised in procurement procedures.

It now appears possible, due to Brexit, that the UK public procurement law regime may experience another revision, as both the European Union (Withdrawal) Act ("EUWA") and the European Commission Draft Withdrawal Agreement[8] ("DWA") are likely to directly impact on UK public procurement law.

- **The European Union (Withdrawal) Act (EUWA)**
  - designed to implement the terms of Brexit and maintain legal certainty
  - repeals the European Communities Act 1972
  - converts much of EU law into domestic law, known as 'retained law'

- **The European Commission Draft Withdrawal Agreement (DWA)**
  - designed to set out the terms of the UK's withdrawal from the EU
  - includes specific provisions addressing procurement law (Title VIII, Articles 71 – 74)

---

7 See Part 4 of Directive 2014/24/EU, Miscellaneous obligations
8 European Commission, Task Force for the Preparation and Conduct of the Negotiations with the United Kingdom under Article 50 TEU, *Draft Agreement on the withdrawal of the United Kingdom of Great Britain and Northern Ireland from the European Union and the European Atomic Energy Community*, (19 March 2018), <https://ec.europa.eu/commission/sites/beta-political/files/draft_agreement_coloured.pdf> accessed 9 May 2018

These two pieces of legislation, currently in draft format, will directly influence the eventual shape of UK procurement law after Brexit. The EUWA will disapply the supremacy of EU law[9], ending the preliminary reference procedure to the CJEU and ensuring that transposed EU procurement law will continue to have effect as domestic law after Exit Day. The DWA will have the most significant impact on the detail of how procurement processes will be run after Exit Day, until 31 December 2020, the ("Transition Period") and, to a limited extent, after the end of the Transition Period.

European Union Withdrawal Act and procurement law

The EUWA states that EU-derived domestic legislation[10] will continue to have effect in domestic law on and after Exit Day.[11] As the PCR 2015 and the CCR 2016 are EU-derived domestic legislation, they will therefore remain in place and continue to have effect after Exit Day.

At the time of writing, it appears that UK procurement law will not continue to be subject to CJEU rulings after the end of the transition period. Section 6, 'Interpretation of retained EU law' of the EUWA[12] states the following:

---

1 A court or tribunal
   a is not bound by any principles laid down, or any decisions made, on or after exit day by the European Court, and
   b cannot refer any matter to the European Court on or after exit day.
2 Subject to this and subsections (3) to (6), a court or tribunal may have regard to anything done on or after exit day by the European Court, another EU entity or the EU so far as it is relevant to any matter before the court or tribunal.

---

9 The European Communities Act 1972, which acts as the 'gateway' for EU legislation in the UK, will be repealed by the EUWA on Exit Day, as part of the process of leaving the EU (as specified by Clause 1 of the EUWA).
10 As it has effect in domestic law immediately before Exit Day
11 European Union (Withdrawal) Act 2018, Section 2(1)
12 European Union (Withdrawal) Act 2018

> 3   Any question as to the validity, meaning or effect of any retained EU law is to be decided, so far as that law is unmodified on or after exit day and so far as they are relevant to it—
>
>   a   in accordance with any retained case law and any retained general principles of EU law, and
>
>   b   having regard (among other things) to the limits, immediately before exit day, of EU competences.
>
> 4   But—
>
>   a   the Supreme Court is not bound by any retained EU case law
>
>   ...
>
> 5   In deciding whether to depart from any retained EU case law, the Supreme Court or the High Court of Justiciary must apply the same test as it would apply in deciding whether to depart from its own case law.

The EUWA demonstrates several key principles. First, that the UK courts will not be bound by the CJEU after Exit Day. Second, after Exit Day, a domestic court may have regard to the CJEU, an EU entity, or the EU, if it is relevant to the matter at hand. Third, interpretations of retained EU law are to be decided in accordance with relevant retained case law and retained EU law principles. Fourth, the Supreme Court may depart from retained EU case law by applying the same test it would apply when determining whether to depart from its own case law.

As can be seen from these provisions, there is scope for the PCR 2015, if it is deemed to fall within the definition of 'retained EU law', to be interpreted in accordance with retained case law and any retained general principles of EU law. This is a useful mechanism which will aid questions of interpretation in situations where Exit Day is relatively recent. However, developments in EU procurement law will continue after Exit Day, whether these are as a result of ongoing case law establishing new principles, whether they are as a result of amendments to the Directives, or if there are new European Commission communications which set out guidelines for the conduct of procurement processes. As time passes, procurement law principles will be refined and elaborated, and new principles will emerge. EU procurement law will continue to develop, and the UK's retained EU procurement law will effectively be frozen in time at the point of departure. The two procurement regimes may take increasingly different paths.

Without a further agreement on procurement law which goes beyond the principles outlined in the EUWA and the DWA, the UK's procurement law regime will, over time, become increasingly incompatible with the EU's procurement regime. If compatibility is to be maintained, the UK would need to make a commitment to being continually bound by the EU's evolving procurement law regime. This commitment would need to include the acceptance of CJEU jurisdiction (and to be bound by principles set out in EU case law), the implementation of the EU's changes to procurement legislation and an agreement to observe EU institution guidance on procurement law issues. Identifying the likely direction of UK procurement law policy is therefore important to ascertain the future shape of EU procurement law.

UK government statements on procurement law policy

In the UK government's technical note in March 2018 on other separation issues (Figure 1.1)[13], public procurement procedures were addressed. It stated, 'The UK's priority is to ensure that public procurement continues to function as smoothly as possible, avoiding disruption to public procurement markets for the benefit of suppliers and procurers'. It also mentioned that the, 'UK aims for an ambitious future relationship on public procurement' and the 'UK will be seeking further reassurances about the ability of UK companies to bid into EU-level procurement exercises organised by the EU institutions before the date of withdrawal, and to be treated equally, without discrimination'. These statements demonstrate awareness of and engagement with the policy objectives of a well-regulated public procurement system, from both the perspective of the purchaser and the provider. However, it remains to be seen how these stated objectives will take shape in practical terms.

---

13 HM Government, *Other Separation Issues - Phase 2*, (Technical note, March 2018), <https://assets.publishing.service.gov.uk/government/uploads/system/uploads/ attachment_data/file/685748/Other_Separation_Issues_Technical_note_ March_2018.pdf> accessed 12 May 2018

> "The UK's priority is to ensure that public procurement continues to function as smoothly as possible, avoiding disruption to public procurement markets for the benefit of suppliers and procurers"

Figure 1.1 Quote from HM Government, Other Separation Issues - Phase 2, (Technical note, March 2018).

Government White Paper and procurement law[14]

The long-awaited Government White Paper published in July 2018 touches on the topic of procurement. It appears to suggest changing the current procurement regime; competition and state aid regimes would remain aligned with the EU, but the procurement regime would not. The White Paper references the intention to develop 'new tailored arrangements' in relation to 'the UK's future public procurement policy' and to push for 'greater liberalisation' of procurement markets. Very few specific details are given, other than the mention of the UK becoming 'a member of the Government Procurement Agreement ("GPA") in its own right', a route the UK pursued in June 2018, when it applied for accession.

European Commission Communication – impact of the 'no deal' scenario on procurement law

The communication issued by the European Commission in July 2018 addressed the possibility of a scenario where the UK and EU are not able to agree the terms of the UK's withdrawal by October 2018, in time for the EU's conclusion process and the UK's ratification process. The communication sets out that if the terms of the DWA are not agreed by October, then the consequence would be the UK leaving

14 HM Government, *The Future Relationship between the United Kingdom and the European Union* (July 2018) <https://assets.publishing.service.gov.uk/government/uploads/system/uploads/attachment_data/file/725288/The_future_relationship_between_the_United_Kingdom_and_the_European_Union.pdf> accessed 16 July 2018

the EU in March 2019 without an agreed trade deal (or a transition period). The communication identifies that in the situation where the UK leaves the EU in March 2019 without a deal, then procurement processes would be impacted;

> UK entities would cease to be eligible as Union entities for the pur-
> pose of receiving EU grants and participating in EU procurement
> procedures. Unless otherwise provided for by the legal provisions
> in force, candidates or tenderers from the United Kingdom could
> be rejected[15]

This anticipates that UK bidders may struggle to be successful in EU procurement procedures or may be rejected outright. However, if the UK's application to accede to the GPA[16] is successful, then, depending on the details of the UK's agreement with the GPA, it is possible that, as a GPA member, the UK may be able to participate in EU procurement processes.[17]

The Irish border and its impact on procurement law

The need to avoid a hard border in Ireland is one of the key Brexit negotiation issues. Currently, both Ireland and Northern Ireland are part of the single market and customs union (with the same regulatory and standards governance). If the UK and Northern Ireland leave the EU by exiting the single market and the customs union, then this will necessitate a hard border where there will potentially be customs duties, or other charges, and, in addition, product standards, food and livestock checks. At first glance the issue of the Irish border appears

---

15 European Commission Communication, *Preparing for the withdrawal of the United Kingdom from the European Union on 30 March 2019*, Brussels, 19.7.2018, COM (2018) 556 final <https://eur-lex.europa.eu/legal-content/EN/TXT/?uri= COM%3A2018%3A556%3AFIN > accessed 15 July 2018

16 Letter from Delegation of the European Union to World Trade Organization Membership containing an application for accession of the United Kingdom to the Agreement on Government Procurement in its own right (1 June 2018) <https:// docs.wto.org/dol2fe/Pages/FE_Search/FE_S_S009-DP.aspx?Language=E& CatalogueIdList=245666,245668,245669,245670,245671,245719,245701,245667,2456 58,245655&CurrentCatalogueIdIndex=5&FullTextHash=371857150> accessed 21 July 2018

17 Public Contracts Regulations 2015 (as amended), Regulation 25, 'contracting au-thorities shall accord to the works, supplies, services and economic operators of the signatories to those agreements treatment no less favourable than the treatment accorded to the works, supplies, services and economic operators of the EU'.

somewhat removed from procurement law, however the outcome of this issue will have a direct impact on procurement law. Arguably, if there is no satisfactory solution to this issue, it will not be possible for the UK to leave the single market. Remaining in the single market will mandate continued acceptance of all EU procurement rules, as explored below.

The Phase 1 Joint Report agreement between the EU and UK, published in early December 2017, contains some conflicting statements in relation to Northern Ireland which are difficult to reconcile.

Paragraph 49 is a key paragraph[18], setting the outline terms for the UK's route to exit in the absence of agreement on the circumstances in Northern Ireland. It states, 'in the absence of agreed solutions[19], the United Kingdom will maintain full alignment with those rules of the Internal Market and the Customs Union which, now or in the future, support North-South cooperation... and the protection of the 1998 [Good Friday] Agreement'.

When attempting to identify a potential solution, the text refers to how, 'The United Kingdom also recalls its commitment to the avoidance of a hard border, including any physical infrastructure or related checks and controls'.[20] Currently, there is no solution where it is possible to have a 'soft' border without maintaining alignment with the rules of the Internal Market and the Customs Union. It appears that if a hard border is to be avoided, then alignment with the Internal Market and the Customs Union would be required.

The March 2018 version of the DWA notes[21] that no agreement has been reached yet on the right operational approach. It states that the

---

18 Negotiators Of The European Union And The United Kingdom Government, *Joint Report On Progress During Phase 1 Of Negotiations Under Article 50 TEU On The United Kingdom's Orderly Withdrawal From The European Union*, (8 December 2017) <https://www.gov.uk/government/uploads/system/uploads/attachment_data/file/665869/Joint_report_on_progress_during_phase_1_of_negotiations_under_Article_50_TEU_on_the_United_Kingdom_s_orderly_withdrawal_from_the_European_Union.pdf> accessed 10 June 2017

19 Emphasis added

20 Negotiators of The European Union And The United Kingdom Government (n19) [43]

21 The DWA displays a note on the first page which states, 'With respect to the Draft Protocol On Ireland/Northern Ireland, the negotiators agree that a legally operative version of the "backstop" solution for the border between Northern Ireland and Ireland, in line with paragraph 49 of the Joint Report, should be agreed as part of the legal text of the Withdrawal Agreement, to apply unless and until another solution is found. The negotiators have reached agreement on some elements of the draft Protocol. They further agree that the full set of issues related to avoiding a hard border covered in the draft reflect

DWA will need to include, as part of its text, the approach described in Paragraph 49 of the Phase 1 agreement, unless or until another solution is found.

The eventual shape of procurement law will be impacted by the 'alignment' (or otherwise) of the UK and EU's regulatory approach. This much debated[22] Phase 1 agreement provides early indications of the issues the UK will have to resolve in order to step away from the single market. Of course, if the UK cannot resolve these issues, then it appears that the UK will stay in the single market and procurement law will remain unchanged.

---

those that need to be addressed in any solution. There is as yet no agreement on the right operational approach, but the negotiators agree to engage urgently in the process of examination of all relevant matters announced on 14 March and now under way', European Commission, Task Force for the Preparation and Conduct of the Negotiations with the United Kingdom under Article 50 TEU, *Draft Agreement on the withdrawal of the United Kingdom of Great Britain and Northern Ireland from the European Union and the European Atomic Energy Community*, (19 March 2018), 1 <https://ec.europa.eu/commission/sites/beta-political/files/draft_agreement_coloured.pdf> accessed 9 May 2018

22 Maïa de La Baume, 'No Brexit transition deal until progress on withdrawal, Guy Verhofstadt says comments from David Davis that agreement is not 'legally enforceable' undermined trust' *Politico* (1 December 2017) <https://www.politico.eu/article/manfred-weber-guy-verhofstadt-eu-parliament-no-brexit-transition-deal-until-progress-on-withdrawal/> accessed 17 July 2018

2 European Commission Draft Withdrawal Agreement and procurement law

Draft Withdrawal Agreement key provisions

Separately from the UK's domestic European Union Withdrawal Act ("EUWA"), the European Commission Draft Withdrawal Agreement ("DWA") is being developed through round table negotiations between the 27 European Union Member States ("EU 27"). The DWA provides for transitional arrangements which will keep EU law in place until 31 December 2020.

Some early thought was given to the procurement law implications of the Transition Period in a position paper towards the end of 2017.[1] Subsequently, an early DWA was then published in February 2018[2] which addressed public procurement at Title VIII. Approximately a month later, a subsequent version of the draft DWA was published,[3] which made some amendments to the procurement-specific provisions. In June 2018, a joint statement was released, which identified that all of

1 European Commission, *Position paper on On-going Public Procurement Procedures, European Commission to UK*, (TF50 (2017) 12/2 20 September 2017), <https://ec.europa.eu/commission/sites/beta-political/files/public_procurement.pdf> accessed 24 July 2017

2 European Commission, *Draft Withdrawal Agreement on the withdrawal of the United Kingdom of Great Britain and Northern Ireland from the European Union and the European Atomic Energy Community, Commission to EU 27*, (28 February 2018 TF50 (2018) 33), Title VIII, <https://ec.europa.eu/commission/sites/beta-political/files/draft_withdrawal_agreement.pdf> accessed 24 July 2017

3 European Commission, *Draft Agreement on the withdrawal of the United Kingdom of Great Britain and Northern Ireland from the European Union and the European Atomic Energy Community*, <https://ec.europa.eu/commission/sites/beta-political/files/draft_agreement_coloured.pdf> 19 March 2018, last accessed 9 May 2018

Table 2.1 Summary of the procurement provisions in Title VIII of the DWA

TITLE VIII **ONGOING PUBLIC PROCUREMENT AND SIMILAR PROCEDURES**	
Article 71 – Definition	Refers to how 'relevant rules' means the general principles of Union law applicable to the award of public contracts and Directives 2014/23/EU and 2014/24/EU[5]
Article 72 – Rules applicable to ongoing procedures	**1(a)** States that the 'relevant rules' shall apply to - Procedures launched by contracting authorities in the UK under the relevant rules before the end of the Transition Period which have not yet been finalised - Includes dynamic purchasing systems - Includes procedures where a PIN is used as a call for competition or periodic indicative notice or a notice on the existence of a qualification system **1(b)** States that the 'relevant rules' shall apply to - Framework agreements concluded before the end of the Transition Period which have not expired or been terminated - Framework agreements concluded after the end of the Transition Period in accordance with a procedure mentioned in 72(1)(a) **2** The non-discrimination principle shall be complied with in relation to the procedures mentioned in 1(a) **3** A procedure mentioned in 72(1)(a) is considered launched when a call for competition or any other invitation to submit applications is made, or when the contracting authority has contacted operators in relation to the competition **4** A procedure is considered finalised when: **a)** A contract award notice is published, or if a contract award notice is not published, when the contract is concluded **b)** If a contract is not to be awarded, when tenderers, or those entitled to apply, are notified why the contract was not awarded

the procurement-specific provisions have been agreed at negotiators' level and are therefore only subject to technical legal revisions.[4]

---

4 Joint statement from the negotiators of the European Union and the United Kingdom Government on progress of negotiations under Article 50 TEU on the United Kingdom's orderly withdrawal from the European Union. (Articles 72(2) & 73) (19 June 2018) <https://ec.europa.eu/commission/sites/beta-political/files/joint_statement.pdf> accessed 24 June 2018

5 Commission Regulation (EC) No 213/2008 of 28 November 2007 amending Regulation (EC) No 2195/2002 of the European Parliament and of the Council on the

The procurement-specific provisions in the section 'Ongoing Public Procurement and Similar Procedures' of the DWA regulate the operation of procurement law during the Transition Period (Table 2.1). The next section of this book analyses the content of these provisions, detailing what legal certainties have been provided, but also exploring the potential meaning of definitions, cut-off dates, ambiguities and lacunae in the drafting.

Analysis of Draft Withdrawal Agreement key provisions

The provisions in the section 'Ongoing Public Procurement and Similar Procedures'[6] raise some questions over how they will operate in practice. The section begins by stating:

> For the purposes of this Title, "relevant rules" means the general principles of Union law applicable to the award of public contracts... (the relevant directives) ... and any other specific rules of Union law governing public procurement procedures.

The reference to the 'general principles of Union law' is most likely to be understood to mean the Treaty principles[7] of free movement of goods, freedom of establishment and the freedom to provide services, as well as the connected principles of equal treatment, non-discrimination, mutual recognition, proportionality and transparency.

It is important that the meaning of this phrase 'general principles of Union law' does encompass procurement-specific case law, so that the body of Court of Justice of the European Union ("CJEU") procurement case law is available to be interpreted until, at the very least, 31 December 2020. This is particularly important for the functionality of EU procurement law, in particular in relation to contracts which will continue to be subject to the EU procurement regime after the expiry of the Transition Period.

Article 4 of the DWA assists with whether the phrase the 'general principles of Union law' is also intended to cover EU case law.

Common Procurement Vocabulary (CPV) and Directives 2004/17/EC and 2004/18/EC of the European Parliament and of the Council on public procurement procedures, as regards the revision of the CPV (Text with EEA relevance) <https://eur-lex.europa.eu/legal-content/EN/TXT/?uri=celex:32008R0213> accessed 22 July 2018

6 ibid Title VIII, Articles 71–74

7 Consolidated version of the Treaty on the Functioning of the European Union [2012], OJ C 326

Article 4

Methods and principles relating to the effect, the implementation and the application of this Agreement

1   The provisions of this Agreement referring to concepts or provisions of Union law shall be interpreted and applied in accordance with the same methods and general principles as those applicable within the Union.
2   The provisions of this Agreement referring to Union law or concepts or provisions thereof shall in their implementation and application be interpreted in conformity with the relevant case law of the Court of Justice of the European Union handed down before the end of the Transition Period.
3   In the interpretation and application of this Agreement, the UK's judicial and administrative authorities shall have due regard to relevant case law of the CJEU handed down after the end of the transition period.

The clarity added by the provisions in Article 4(3) and 4(4) is crucial. Many of the key principles of procurement law can only be fully understood by a review of the history of the case law on that topic and an understanding of the current position according to the CJEU. Article 4(5) uses the phrase 'authorities shall have due regard' in relation to how authorities should approach case law after the Transition Period ends. As set out below, there will be some contracts which will still be subject to the EU procurement rules after the end of the Transition Period. It remains to be seen how the notion of 'due regard' will take shape in practical terms when procurement decisions are made in relation to these 'legacy' contracts.

Contracts subject to the EU procurement regime after the Transition Period

There will be certain contracts which will continue to be subject to the EU procurement regime even after the expiry of the Transition Period. This is due to the drafting in relation to the rules applicable to ongoing procedures and the definitions of when a contract is 'launched' and when it is 'finalised'. The provisions have the effect of gradually decreasing the impact of the EU public procurement regime over a period of time. New procurement procedures commenced after the end of the Transition Period will not be impacted by EU public procurement law, but for some years after the end of the Transition Period there will continue to be contracts which are regulated by the relevant rules. The uncertainty over whether the phrase 'relevant rules' refers just to the Treaty on the Functioning of the European Union principles and to Directives 2014/24 and 2014/23, or whether this phrase also refers to CJEU case law, is likely to be addressed during the Transition Period.

Procurement procedures ongoing at the end of the Transition Period

Article 72 DWA, 'Rules applicable to ongoing procedures' specifies that for some framework agreements and also for some call-off contracts from framework agreements, EU law could continue to apply for some time after the end of the Transition Period.

It specifies that EU procurement law applies to certain procurement processes which have been commenced by contracting authorities before 31 December 2020 but have not yet completed. This includes procurement processes for dynamic purchasing systems, as well as 'procedures for which the call for competition takes the form of a prior information notice or periodic indicative notice or a notice on the existence of a qualification system'. It also incorporates framework agreements. It makes provision in respect of framework agreements which have been procured, but which continue to be operational at the end of the Transition Period.

These are most likely to be contracts which were launched close to the end of the Transition Period. Article 72(1)(a) provides that the relevant rules shall apply to procurement processes launched before the end of the Transition Period which have not yet been finalised. Articles 72(3) and (4) offer some additional definitions to provide clarity in respect of what is intended by the terms 'launched'[8] and 'finalised'[9]. A procedure is launched when a call for competition or any other invitation to submit applications has been made, or if these specific formalities are

---

8 European Commission, *Draft Withdrawal Agreement on the withdrawal of the United Kingdom of Great Britain and Northern Ireland from the European Union and the European Atomic Energy Community*, 28 February 2018 TF50 (2018) 33 – Commission to EU 27 - Article 72 (3), <https://ec.europa.eu/commission/sites/beta-political/files/draft_withdrawal_agreement.pdf> last accessed 9 May 2018
9 ibid Article 72(4)

not required, then 'the procedure shall be considered launched when the contracting authority or contracting entity has contacted economic operators in relation to the specific procedure'. The DWA includes specific rules in relation to when a procedure is considered finalised, when a contract award notice is published (or, if a contract award notice is not required, on conclusion of the relevant contract), or when applicants and tenderers are informed why the contract was not awarded.

It also legislates for framework agreements which have not yet concluded at the end of the Transition Period. Interestingly, as call-off contracts on framework agreements may extend beyond the term of the framework agreement (which is a maximum of four years[10]), this could potentially mean that EU procurement law continues to apply to these contracts for some years after the Transition Period has concluded.

DWA and equality under procurement law

The principle of non-discrimination is a provision which goes to the heart of the EU procurement law principle of equal treatment. The key issue is whether, during the Transition Period, the UK will continue to treat tenderers from other EU member states equally to domestic tenderers. This provision in Article 72(2)[11] was one of the last in Title VIII to be agreed (it is now only subject to technical legal revisions). On the basis of this provision, during the Transition Period, the UK will be obliged to treat all tenderers, regardless of their member state affiliation, equally. While the principle of equal treatment is arguably inherent in the 'general principles of Union law' referred to above, it appears that it is of sufficient importance for explicit attention to be drawn to this particular policy consideration. The UK will also need to observe this principle in relation to procurement procedures which are commenced during the Transition Period but are finalised subsequent to the Transition Period end date, another example of how EU obligations will continue past the end of the Transition Period.

DWA and modification of existing contracts

The DWA does not explicitly address issues of contract modification during the Transition Period. Arguably, modification of contracts may be covered by the DWA's catch-all reference to 'general principles of

---

10 Public Contracts Regulations 2015 (as amended), Regulation 33(3)

11 ibid Article 72(2)

Union law'. This reference could be interpreted to mean that the modification of contracts should be approached in the way it is currently approached, under the general principles of Union law.

It is possible that the view of the negotiators when drafting the DWA was that it is not practical to refer in detail to a number of different provisions and therefore the phrase 'general principles of Union law' would serve as an umbrella term to cover a number of different procurement law considerations.

In the context of the modification of existing contracts, it is unclear whether the phrase 'general principles of Union law' would refer to Article 72, 'Modification of contracts during their term'[12] or to the transposed Regulation 72[13]. Presumably, due to the reference to 'Union law', it would relate to the EU source text of Article 72.

Additionally, perhaps it is unlikely that there will be a large number of contracts which fall into the group of contracts to which the rules about contract modification would be relevant. It may not have been seen as necessary to amplify this particular consideration with a dedicated provision. For a contract to fall into this group, it would need to be a contract which was procured prior to the end of the Transition Period and requires modification after the end of the Transition Period.

The lack of clarity on this topic could lead to unintended outcomes. For example, contracting authorities procuring towards the end of the Transition Period and anticipating that a contract may need to vary its scope and/or scale across the term of the contract may change their procurement strategy. Procuring a scalable contract from the outset typically requires a lengthier and more complex procurement process and a more sophisticated tender structure and assessment approach. It entails more detailed pricing models and a wide range of quality questions at tender stage. If the contract is to be scalable during the contract term without attracting procurement risk then it will need to include clear, precise and unequivocal review clauses (which may include price revision clauses or options) and clauses which state the scope and nature of possible modifications or options as well as the conditions under which they may be used. This degree of planning during the procurement process requires significant resource.

If, towards the end of the Transition Period, it appears that there is no certainty that EU procurement contract modification rules will

---

12 Directive 2014/24/EU, Article 72, Modification of contracts during their term
13 Public Contracts Regulations 2015 (as amended), Regulation 72

continue to apply after the end of the Transition Period, then contracting authorities may adapt their procurement strategy. They may be tempted to procure only the work needed at the outset of the contract and modify the contract after the end of the Transition Period. Of course, if a contracting authority were to do this, it would present some risk. An arrangement could be reached with the EU at the last moment, and more importantly Regulation 72 of the Public Contracts Regulations 2015 ("PCR 2015") would still apply, meaning that a complainant could present a case on the basis of a breach of the domestic procurement legislation.

While it would evidently not have been practical for the DWA to explicitly reference many different types of provisions, contract modification is one of the more significant procurement issues which arises. Detailing how this issue should be approached would have aided clarity.

Procurement complaints under the DWA

The discussion of contract modification leads on to the area of procurement complaints. A procurement breach occurring during the Transition Period would be brought on the basis that the 'relevant rules' mentioned in the DWA apply to the contract in question. The exact meaning of the 'relevant rules' would need to be determined before the complaint or challenge could successfully proceed. Another possibility is that a breach could occur during the time period covered by the DWA, however the complaint or challenge could be brought after the expiry of this time period. In this second scenario, it is not yet known what rules will apply; that will be decided as part of the UK's as yet undetermined exit arrangements.

Looking into the future

The DWA does not offer any direction on the eventual shape of public procurement for procedures commenced after the Transition Period end date. This leaves a regulatory lacuna. At the time of writing, procurement procedures which commence after the Transition Period (and procured contracts which require modification after the Transition Period) will only be regulated by the PCR 2015 and Concession Contracts Regulations 2016 ("CCR 2016"). The most likely outcome is that something new will need to be created to fill this regulatory vacuum.

Currently, there is significant cross-border procurement (direct and indirect), and this has increased in recent years, to around 23% of the total value of procurement in the EU.[14] If the UK was not able to participate in the cross-border procurement market after Brexit, this would have an economic impact. The outcome for procurement law after the Transition Period largely depends on the shape of the deal agreed between the UK and the EU. The closer the regulatory alignment agreed in the deal is, the stronger the likelihood that procurement law will remain unchanged and identical to the EU system. For procurement law to continue to be aligned with the EU's procurement regime, UK procurement law needs to continue to be subject to CJEU rulings and for any new directives, or amendments to the current Directives, to require implementation by the UK. At the end of the Transition Period EU and UK procurement law will be identical. However, if UK procurement law is not part of the EU procurement regime in the future, the differences between the two will become increasingly noticeable as time passes. If amendments to EU directives are not transposed and EU case law is not observed, after some years, the UK and EU procurement regimes may look very different indeed.

---

14 Communication from the Commission to the European Parliament, the Council, the European Economic and Social Committee and the Committee of the Regions, *Making Public Procurement work in and for Europe*, Strasbourg, 3.10.2017, COM(2017) 572 final, 4 <http://eur-lex.europa.eu/legal-content/EN/TXT/PDF/?uri=CELEX:52017DC0572&from=EN> accessed 26 May 2018

3 Losing access to EU online tools, universal classification systems and other guidance

There are several key online tools or common classification systems used during procurement processes which the UK currently benefits from – eCertis, Official Journal of the European Union ("OJEU") advertising and Common Procurement Vocabulary ("CPV") codes. The loss of these may affect the ease with which the UK can advertise and procure its contracts.

eCertis and the European Single Procurement Document

eCertis is an online information system which holds the documents needed to participate in cross-border tendering in each Member State. Member States currently voluntarily update the system as required with the needed documents. In the PCR 2015, the use of eCertis is delayed to 18 October 2018[1]. After that date, Member States will be required to keep eCertis updated, with contracting authorities primarily requiring documentary evidence covered by eCertis[2]. One of the functions of eCertis is that it can be used to supply European Single Procurement Documents ("ESPDs").

The concept of the ESPD is that it should be a single source of information for procuring authorities to receive confirmation that suppliers meet the exclusion and selection criteria. Suppliers can provide a link to online document repositories where this information can be verified.

The use of eCertis for documentary evidence for procurement procedures which are ongoing at the Transition Period end date can continue for an additional nine months after the end date. The European

---

1 Public Contracts Regulations (as amended), Regulation 1 (5)
2 Directive 2014/24/EU, Article 61(2).

Commission Draft Withdrawal Agreement ("DWA") states that this provision 'shall apply for a period not exceeding 9 months from the end of the Transition Period in respect of the procedures under that Directive launched by contracting authorities from the United Kingdom before the end of the Transition Period and not yet finalised on the last day thereof'.[3] There is a clear cut off at the end of the nine months.

It is not currently clear to what extent UK bidders will still be able to participate in EU procurement processes after the end of the Transition Period. However, if UK bidders wish to continue to participate in EU procurement processes after UK access to eCertis has been terminated (i.e. after the nine-month period mentioned above), they will not be able to use eCertis to supply an ESPD. UK bidders will therefore need to find an alternative method of providing data to prove their compliance with the exclusion and selection criteria.

If UK bidders need to find an alternative method of providing data or documentation, this may place them at a disadvantage when compared to bidders from the EU. While this issue will not affect the assessment of their response to either the selection or award stage, it may well place an extra administrative burden on UK suppliers when they are participating in EU procurement processes. They will be unable to provide information in the standardised format that EU bidders will be able to, via EU bidders' continued use of eCertis. It appears that the use of the ESPD[4] will become increasingly commonplace in EU procurement processes as acceptance of ESPD self-declaration forms is mandated by Directive 2014/24, although different member states will have chosen different implementation dates. UK bidders may therefore be faced with a more onerous task; they may not be able to reuse the ESPD for multiple procurements in the way that EU bidders will be able to.

3 European Commission, *Draft Withdrawal Agreement on the withdrawal of the United Kingdom of Great Britain and Northern Ireland from the European Union and the European Atomic Energy Community*, 19 March 2018 TF50 (2018) 33 – Commission to EU 27 - Article 74 (3), <https://ec.europa.eu/commission/sites/beta-political/files/draft_agreement_coloured.pdf> accessed 9 May 2018

4 European Commission, *European Single Procurement Document* (ESPD) Tools, <https://ec.europa.eu/tools/espd/filter?lang=en> and, *European Single Procurement Document and eCertis, Growth, Internal Market, Industry, Entrepreneurship and SMEs*, <https://ec.europa.eu/growth/single-market/public-procurement/e-procurement/espd_en> both accessed 28 May 2018

Official Journal of the European Union advertising

The ability to advertise in the "OJEU" may well be removed. The UK currently has a domestic procurement advertising function, known as Contracts Finder, which, under the Public Contracts Regulations 2015 ("PCR 2015"), contracting authorities are obliged to use when procuring contracts of prescribed values.[5] Therefore, when considering alternative options to OJEU advertising, there is already a starting point for a domestic advertising model. The original aim behind Contracts Finder was to promote greater transparency in commercial activity, demonstrating the UK government's commitment to probity in relation to the use of public funds and transparency in relation to procurement decision-making processes. Additionally, requiring the publication of some below threshold contracts in Contracts Finder supports the aim of making the public procurement market more accessible to SMEs, a policy objective embodied by the Lord Young procurement reforms.

To this end, currently contracting authorities (with some minor exceptions) are required to publish not only information in relation to above EU threshold contracts but also information in relation to some contracts below the mandatory EU advertising thresholds and to comply with certain requirements in relation to assessing the suitability of candidates.[6,7]

Common Procurement Vocabulary codes

The universality of the CPV codes,[8] across EU member states, provides a useful classification system for procuring authorities to categorise and advertise the types of works, services and goods they require when procuring contracts. Similarly, this classification system offers suppliers the potential to register against alerts for specific CPV codes of interest. As CPV codes are available in all of the EU's official

---

5 The statutory requirements in respect of Contracts Finder are set out in Regulations 106 - 112 Public Contracts Regulations 2015 (as amended).

6 At the time of writing, updated thresholds can be found at: <https://www.ojec.com/thresholds.aspx>

7 The explanatory note in the Public Contracts Regulations 2015 (as amended) summarises the effect of Part 4, which contains the domestic Contracts Finder obligations

8 European Commission, 'Single Market and Standards, Common Procurement Vocabulary', <https://ec.europa.eu/growth/single-market/public-procurement/rules-implementation/common-vocabulary_en≥ accessed 28 May 2018

languages[9], this system helps to facilitate cross-border procurement, as suppliers can identify tender notices through use of the universal CPV code system.

In a survey carried out for a report in 2012, the conclusion was that 'of the contracting authorities surveyed, 70% thought that the codes allow more bidders to become aware of their notices and 56% stated that the CPV leads to better value for money. Of the bidders surveyed, 57% stated that the CPV allows them to become aware of more tender notices, and 45% perceived that the CPV leads to more business opportunities'[10]. If this system was not accessible to either procuring authorities or suppliers, this would reduce the ease of access to advertised cross-border contracts for suppliers based outside the UK and consequently reduce contracting authorities' choice of suppliers. It appears that on exiting the EU, the UK may cease to use CPV codes, as there has been no statement to the contrary and there does not, at present, appear to be an identified replacement which will act as a universally accessible classification system.

Loss of EU Directive 2014/24 and 2014/23 recitals

When there is ambiguity in relation to certain provisions of the PCR 2015 or Concession Contracts Regulations 2016 ("CCR 2016"), then the recitals to each Directive are a useful source of interpretation. For example, in the case of the CCR 2016, Directive 2014/23 sheds some light on how to identify a concession contract, explaining, 'difficulties related to the interpretation of the concepts of concession and public contract have generated continued legal uncertainty among stakeholders and have given rise to numerous judgments of the Court of Justice of the European Union. Therefore, the definition of concession should be clarified, in particular by referring to the concept of operating risk'. For issues such as these, the presence of recitals can offer an important aid to interpretation. However, neither the PCR 2015 or CCR 2016 contain the recitals, they are only contained at the front of the original Directives.

There is an unanswered question in relation to whether domestic courts will have recourse to the recitals when they have not been made

---

9 European Commission, DG Internal Market and Services, *Final Report, Review of the Functioning of the CPV codes/system, MARKT/2011/111/C*, December 2012, 10 <http://ec.europa.eu/DocsRoom/documents/21583/attachments/1/translations> accessed 28 May 2018

10 ibid 10.

available in the transposed legislation. If the recitals are not viewed as part of the legislation, it is possible that the UK's conceptual understanding of key EU public procurement concepts, which would have been enhanced by the presence of the recitals, will begin to diverge from EU intentions.

In conclusion, there are a number of tools which the UK may lose access to, some of these may be a significant loss (such as the loss of CPV codes to identify contracts). For others, it may be possible to further develop already existing domestic functions, such as Contracts Finder. In respect of the Recitals to the Directives, practitioners and the UK courts may be able to consider these.

Timeline

Figure 3.1 Transition Period timeline.

4 Reduction of access to procurement markets

International procurement instrument

A deterrent against the UK diverging from the EU's procurement rules is the EU's proposed International Procurement Instrument. The European Commission aims to put in place measures to allow the EU to close its public procurement markets to states that do not allow reciprocal and enforceable access to their own public procurement markets.[1] This would encourage the UK to maintain a regulatory procurement regime which is largely comparable to the EU's current legislation, so that market access can be maintained. There is no precise date for when exactly the proposed measures might take effect. The European Commission's proposal aims to incentivise non-EU countries to open up their public procurement markets.

If the UK closed its procurement markets to the EU then, as a third country (having left the EU), it would be subject to the sanctions brought in under the International Procurement Instrument. Under this proposal, in its current draft form, incentivisation methods would apply to 'third' countries (a category the UK is likely to fall within if it leaves the EU) which operate restrictive procurement practices in their markets that discriminate against EU businesses. Two choices would be offered to the third country in question, either the discriminatory practice should be removed, or, when the country bids in EU procurements, a price penalty of up to a 20% increase on the price of

1 European Commission, *Amended proposal for a Regulation of the European Parliament and of the Council on the access of third-country goods and services to the Union's internal market in public procurement and procedures supporting negotiations on access of Union goods and services to the public procurement markets of third countries*, Brussels, 29.1.2016, COM(2016) 34 final, 2012/0060 (COD) <http://trade.ec.europa.eu/doclib/docs/2016/january/tradoc_154187.pdf> accessed 22 July 2018

the submitted tender would apply. This would mean that the bid was placed at a competitive disadvantage. The price penalties would not apply to contracts below €5,000,000, SMEs or developing countries.[2]

If the UK restricts access to its procurement markets, for example, by favouring national bidders, this would pose a challenge to UK businesses. UK business would either be deterred by the price penalties, or they would need to submit proportionally lower prices to overcome the percentage penalty to be applied to their submitted price, absorbing the corresponding profit reduction. Consequently, there is likely to be an observable negative economic impact on UK business who bid in EU procurement processes if the UK diverges from the EU procurement rules.

Practicalities of reduced competition

The possibility of having a separate procurement regime for trade with the EU would add complexity and confusion for both contracting authorities and bidders, illustrated by the example below.

Hypothetical scenario: UK widget seller

A UK SME[3] creates widgets. It sells these widgets to a number of UK contracting authorities, engaging in the UK's domestic procurement process. The SME has employed bid manager staff who have experience navigating the UK Contracts Finder portal, which in the post-Brexit world is the centralised advertising hub for procuring goods, services and works contracts of all values. The SME knows that there are only a few suppliers in the UK who manufacture widgets of the type needed and therefore its goods are in demand.

There are a large number of suppliers who sell almost identical widgets in Germany and France, however they do not tend to bid in UK procurements. The bid manager staff in the German and French businesses primarily monitor the Official Journal of the

---

2 European Commission, 'Press release, European Commission Takes Action to Open Up International Procurement Markets' (Brussels, 29 January 2016) <http://europa.eu/rapid/press-release_IP-16-178_en.htm> accessed 22 July 2018
3 Small and medium-sized enterprise

European Union ("OJEU") adverts, as that is where the majority of the procurement opportunities arise. The adverts on the UK Contracts Finder portal do not come to their attention as frequently. The German and French businesses have occasionally previously bid in UK widget procurements, however they found that it was much more time consuming and expensive to navigate the UK bidding process, they were not able to submit a European Single Procurement Document and they were unfamiliar with the UK procurement process rules.

Therefore, there is only a small market of limited competition. This means that the UK suppliers who do sell widgets have not found that they are frequently being undercut by or outbid by other suppliers and they are accustomed to the quality and price of their product being acceptable to procuring authorities. If the German and French suppliers were to bid, the UK supplier would realise that it has to think more carefully about the competitiveness of its widgets. Consequently, UK contracting authorities who buy widgets find that they continue to receive expensive widgets of only moderate quality

While this is a hypothetical scenario, it illustrates the negative commercial impact of reduced competition. Reduced competition is a likely consequence of the UK departing from EU practices of OJEU advertisement and use of eCertis. It should be noted that this hypothetical example does not address the added detrimental commercial impact that could be caused by the UK closing certain sectors of its procurement market to EU bidders, nor does it address the practical difficulties of operating two differing procurement regimes simultaneously.

Opportunities

5 Potential trading models and their impact on UK procurement

Trading models summary

The procurement regulation which the UK would be subject to in the event of an EU exit largely depends on the type of trading relationship the UK maintains with the EU. There are a few potential trading 'models' which could be emulated in the developing EU-UK relationship (Tables 5.1 and 5.2). An analysis of these models offers guidance as to how UK procurement regulation could develop if one of these models were to be adopted. The trading model which aligns most closely with the current EU procurement regime is the European Economic Area ("EEA") model, in which the UK would largely retain the same procurement regime. Other models include the European Free Trade Association ("EFTA") model and a model based on the EU's trade arrangement with Canada[1]. There is also the World Trade Organisation's ("WTO") Government Procurement Agreement ("GPA"), which offers a more lightly regulated option, with some recognisable key principles. Examining the EU's procurement arrangements with Turkey and Ukraine also offers a perspective on potential future arrangements.

EEA and EFTA State procurement model

EEA membership and the UK's current membership status

The UK currently enjoys EEA membership as an adjunct to its EU membership (as Article 128 of the EEA Agreement[2] states that EU members must also apply to become a party to the EEA). However, there are some unresolved issues in relation to the UK's EEA

---

1 European Commission, Comprehensive Economic and Trade Agreement in Focus, <http://ec.europa.eu/trade/policy/in-focus/ceta/index_en.htm> accessed 22 July 2017

2 Agreement on the European Economic Area [2016] OJ L 1

Table 5.1 Existing trading models and their impact on EU-UK procurement law

	Trading models	Example	Key aspects in relation to EU-UK procurement
1	EEA – European Economic Area	Norway	Free movement is required EEA members are able to sign their own bilateral agreements EU procurement law would be observed
2	EFTA – European Free Trade Association	Switzerland	A few procurement law principles recognisable from the EU procurement law approach However, a fragmented procurement law system with some key differences
3	Free Trade Agreement – bespoke	Canada	Recognisable GPA principles An intention to strengthen the remedies provisions in the future
4	World Trade Organisation, Government Procurement Agreement	Japan	GPA contains recognisable procurement law principles, however remedies rules are less prescriptive No supranational court for individuals, disputes resolved by negotiation
5	UK Ukraine DCFTA	Ukraine	Ukraine is adopting the EU procurement directives and will have a good amount of sector coverage (apart from defence procurement)
6	Turkey model	Turkey	Turkey has customs union arrangements with the EU Currently Turkey's procurement markets are not open to the EU, although this is proposed
7	No identified procurement regime	The laws of most countries regulate government procurement to some extent	Case law and/or judicial review will need to fill the gap The UK is likely to be subject to the EU's international procurement instrument which will close EU public procurement markets to states not allowing reciprocal access to their own public procurement markets

Table 5.2 Potential future trade agreements and their procurement law
implications

UK concludes trade agreements with:	Procurement Law implications
EU	The EU is likely to require compliance with EU procurement regulation. If this is not agreed, it may impose third party sanctions under the International Procurement Instrument
US	The TTIP agreement is envisaged to have in depth coverage of government procurement markets[3], if this approach is emulated there is a possibility that the UK may have a highly regulated UK procurement market in order to offer reciprocal access to the US. This is of course contingent on any trade deal to be negotiated.
Canada	CETA is a model which shows that Canada may be willing to offer access to government procurement markets; the CETA agreement demonstrates for the first time[4] that Canada is willing to offer access to its federal, provincial and municipal markets. Canada has also agreed to publish all contract opportunities on a single website to enhance information access. If this model were to be followed the UK would enjoy a reasonable level of access to Canada's procurement markets.

membership. Article 127 of the EEA Agreement states that a departing EU member state needs to give 12 months' notice when departing from the EU to also leave the EEA. It appears that if the UK does not give notice under Article 127 of the EEA Agreement then it will remain in the EEA (and therefore in the single market, observing the EU procurement regime). If the 12-month notice period is calculated based on the current Exit Day date, then the date by which notice should have been given has already passed, on 29 March 2018. The other option is that, based on the end of the Transition Period being 31 December 2020, the UK could give notice by 31 December 2019 in order to leave the EEA and therefore the single market.

---

3 European Commission, 'Factsheet on Public Procurement in TTIP' (14 July 2016) <http://trade.ec.europa.eu/doclib/docs/2015/january/tradoc_153000.3%20Public %20Procurement.pdf> accessed 12 June 2018

4 European Commission, *Will EU firms be able to bid for public contracts in Canada?* <http://ec.europa.eu/trade/policy/in-focus/ceta/ceta-explained/index_en.htm# public-contracts> accessed 22 July 2018

The UK government's view is that sending the Article 50 letter to leave the EU on 29 March 2017 amounted to implicit notice of leaving the EEA[5] (and therefore triggering the EEA Agreement Article 127 provisions is not required). At the time of writing, the UK government has stated that the UK will be leaving the single market.

Although the UK has not given notice to leave the EEA, as the UK government objects to retaining the four freedoms, it is most likely that the UK will find a method of leaving the EEA around the time of the Transition Period.

However, there remains a small chance that negotiations with the EU could reach a stage where the UK does not decide to leave the single market. Perhaps, in this scenario, the lack of notification to the EEA could work to the UK's advantage. In this situation it would be possible to argue that the UK has not formally left the EEA. If this argument was successful, the UK would remain part of the single market and procurement law would remain unchanged.

EEA membership and the UK's future membership status

The Norwegian model allows access to the EU single market to non-EU member states by means of membership of the EEA[6]. Iceland and Liechtenstein are also EEA members. As well as being EEA members, Iceland, Liechtenstein and Norway are EFTA members (as is Switzerland). EFTA is an intergovernmental body to promote free trade and economic integration.

Currently, the UK is an EEA member (by virtue of being an EU member state), but not an EFTA member. There is no precedent for a country being an EEA member without also being either an EU member state or an EFTA member. If the UK wishes to remain part of the

---

5 House of Commons Research briefing, *The European Economic Area*, (House of Commons Library, Number 8129, June 6 2018) <https://researchbriefings. parliament.uk/ResearchBriefing/Summary/CBP-8129> accessed 11 June 2018

6 European Economic Area (EEA) The Agreement on the European Economic Area, entered into force on 1 January 1994. It comprises both the EU Member States and the three EEA EFTA States (Iceland, Liechtenstein and Norway), forming a single market which is referred to as the Internal Market.

The EEA Agreement ("the Agreement") requires the four freedoms (the free movement of goods, services, persons and capital) throughout the 31 EEA States. The Agreement also covers cooperation in other important areas and guarantees equal rights and obligations for economic operators in the EEA Internal Market.

EFTA, 'The European Free Trade Association' (*EFTA website*): <http://www. efta.int/eea/eea-agreement> accessed 11 June 2018

EEA while leaving the EU, it is most likely that it will need to seek out the opportunity to be an EFTA member.

In order to be part of the EEA, free movement is required, which, at the time of writing, is a red line for the UK government. However, the UK may see it as an advantage that EEA members are able to sign their own bilateral agreements (unlike full EU members, who have to negotiate trade deals as part of the EU).

In practical terms, if the UK were to look to join EFTA, then Iceland, Norway, Switzerland and Liechtenstein would need to agree (and Switzerland would be likely to require a referendum on this topic).

EEA procurement regulation and key principles

If a model similar to the Norwegian EFTA model is adopted, with the UK becoming an EFTA state, then full compliance with EU law which affects the single market would need to be observed. This would include the EU's public procurement directives and relevant Treaty of the Functioning of the European Union principles. In this situation, it would be expected that there would be no changes to the UK's current EU public procurement legislation.[7]

At the heart of the EEA agreement[8] is Article 1, which contains the recognisable principle of free movement, a principle which is familiar from the UK's experience of EU membership. At the time of writing, the UK government's stance is that it will not accept freedom of movement (persons), therefore it appears that this is not a realistic option for the UK.

EEA procurement regulation and preliminary references

In EFTA countries, preliminary references are made to the EFTA Court rather than the Court of Justice of the European Union ("CJEU"). EFTA court cases confirm that many EU procurement principles apply to EEA procurements. In *Casino Admiral AG v Egger*[9], (a case concerning a service concession), it was confirmed that transparency principles

---

7 Agreement on the European Economic Area [1994] OJ L1/Annex XVI
8 Agreement on the European Economic Area [1994] OJ L1/3
9 Case E-24/13, *Casino Admiral AG v Wolfgang Egger* [2014], <http://www.eftacourt.
   int/fileadmin/user_upload/Files/Cases/2013/24_13/24_13_Judgment_EN.pdf>
   accessed 11 June 2018, para 52.

similar to those in the case of *Telaustria*[10] apply to EEA procurements. The court found that the:

> obligation of transparency requires the concession-granting authority to ensure, for the benefit of any potential concessionaire, a degree of advertising sufficient to enable the bid process for the service concession to be opened up to competition and the impartiality of the award procedures to be reviewed[11].

EEA procurement law principles appear similar to EU principles. There are principles of impartiality (equal treatment and lack of bias) and sufficient and transparent advertising to allow interested economic operators to access opportunities.

If the UK were to remain an EEA member, there would be no significant change to the principles underpinning the UK's current procurement law. There may be more opportunities to ask for preliminary references and receive a rapid response, as the EFTA court has the capacity to process cases quickly.

EEA procurement regulation and control over new legislation

Becoming an EFTA member would mean that the UK would have less control over EU legislation than at present. EEA states are involved in the proposal stage of the legislation (committee stage), however they do not have veto rights over legislation and do not play a formal role in EU decision-making. The UK would have a limited degree of influence over the drafting of any new directives and would need to accept any new procurement law legislation.

EFTA procurement model

Switzerland is neither an EU nor EEA member, but is an EFTA[12] member and part of the single market.

---

10 C-324/98 *Telaustria and Telefonadress* [2000] ECR I-10745

11 Case E-24/13, *Casino Admiral AG v Wolfgang Egger* [2014], <http://www.eftacourt. int/fileadmin/user_upload/Files/Cases/2013/24_13/24_13_Judgment_EN.pdf> accessed 11 June 2018, para 52.

12 EFTA.int, 'The European Free Trade Association', <http://www.efta.int/about-efta/ european-free-trade-association> accessed 12 June 2018

Trade arrangements

Access to the EU is governed by a series of over 120 bilateral agreements which cover many areas of trade. The main agreement is the Free Trade Agreement of 1972, and there are a series of sectoral agreements between Switzerland and the EU.

Procurement regulation

Switzerland does have a detailed system of procurement regulation (although it is not subject to EU procurement directives).[13] It is a highly fragmented system, partially due to its evolution over time and partially due to the large variety of cantonal regulation. International legislation plays a part, with Switzerland being a member of the Government Procurement Agreement ("GPA"). Some of the legislation enacted by Switzerland has been put in place with a view to implementing GPA obligations; some legislation regulates federal procurement and some legislation regulates regional and local authorities.

There are some similarities to EU procurement, for example, the principles of transparency and effective competition. Other principles are absent; not all legislation contains a definition of 'contracting authority', instead listing authorities to which procurement legislation applies. The EU procurement law concept of self-cleaning (effectively a defence mechanism to exclusions for misconduct) is unknown, with a more blanket approach to disqualification being adopted. If tenders by foreign bidders are not covered by international procurement obligations then the tender falls to be considered based on whether their home state grants reciprocity.[14]

---

13 Federal Act of Public Procurement of December 16 1994 (as amended) (SR 172.056.1), Federal Ordinance of Public Procurement of December 11 1995 (SR 172.056.11). Regional and local authorities are regulated by the Intercantonal Agreement on Public Procurement of November 25 1994/March 15 2001 and other cantonal public procurement regulations.

There are also international agreements, the Government Procurement Agreement of April 15 1994, the Bilateral Agreement between the European Community and Switzerland on certain aspects of public procurement of June 21 1999 and the Convention establishing the European Free Trade Association of January 4 1960

14 Getting the Deal Through, 'Public Procurement: Switzerland' (July 2017) <https://gettingthedealthrough.com/area/33/jurisdiction/29/public-procurement-switzerland/> accessed 6 July 2018

As the Swiss approach is fragmented, it is an unlikely model for adoption. If the UK were to change its procurement regulation, it is more likely to select one comprehensive approach and implement that.

Canadian procurement model

Trade arrangements

Canada's trading relationship with Europe is due to take the shape of a free trade deal[15], the Comprehensive Economic and Trade Agreement ("CETA"). It has taken approximately seven years to negotiate. On 21 September 2017, CETA entered into force provisionally and therefore at the time of writing, most of the agreement now applies. However, national (and some regional) parliaments in EU member states will need to approve CETA before it can take full effect and its practical impact can be seen. If the UK were to pursue a similar trade deal, then the likelihood, based on the precedent set with Canada, is that this would take some time to negotiate. Therefore, in the short term, the status of procurement law would need to be determined by interim arrangements.

CETA will deliver a high level of access to the single market in goods; 98% of EU goods will enter Canada free of tariffs and duties. However, it excludes some key areas such as services (including financial services), which would not appeal to the UK government. There is no obligation to accept freedom of movement, which would suit the UK government's policy aims.

Procurement regulation

EU companies will be permitted to bid for public procurement contracts in Canada, including those procured by local governments, although there are some limitations with regard to energy utilities.

At the time when the EU and Canada began discussions on the likelihood of a new bilateral agreement, in 2008 and 2009, both parties clearly identified the importance of procurement obligations as a part of the agreement.[16] Chapter 19 of CETA covers government

15 European Commission, CETA – Summary of the final negotiating results <http://trade.ec.europa.eu/doclib/docs/2014/december/tradoc_152982.pdf> accessed 21.7.16, 13

16 Global Affairs Canada, Canada-European Union Joint Report: Towards a Comprehensive Economic Agreement <http://www.international.gc.ca/trade-agreements-

procurement.[17] The Scoping Group which met during the CETA negotiations 'took the view that the starting point on procedural commitments should be the November 2007 revised text of the Government
Procurement Agreement.'[18] The shape of this procurement regulation
(procedures, transparency and information, eligibility, administrative
and judicial remedies) is based on provisions derived from the GPA.
Consequently, the drafting terminology used in the GPA is recognisable; it mirrors GPA references to treatment no less favourable than the
treatment the party in question accords to its own goods, services and
suppliers.[19] Other concepts addressed in the government procurement
chapter are familiar from EU procurement regulation. These concepts
include qualification of suppliers, the ability for suppliers to offer
technical specifications which demonstrate equivalence, transparency
of and advance notice of evaluation criteria, the setting of proportion-
ate time frames for the receipt of tenders, reduction of time periods in
situations of urgency, equal treatment of suppliers in relation to late
tenders, publication of award information, disclosure of information
and review procedures.

One notable provision is the commitment in Article 19.17 that
within a time period of ten years, the parties will take up negotiations to further develop the quality of remedies, including a possible
commitment to introduce or maintain pre-contractual remedies. The
remedies provisions in the Public Contracts Regulations 2015 ("PCR
2015") contain both pre-contractual and post-contractual remedies,
and it appears that the remedies provisions in the government procurement chapter of CETA are not as sophisticated. If the CETA procurement model were to be adopted by the UK, access to remedies for
complainants would not be as developed as the current EU procurement approach.

accords-commerciaux/agr-acc/eu-ue/can-eu-report-can-ue-rapport.aspx?lang=
eng> last edited: 2012.04.13 accessed 22 July 2017

17 Government of Canada, 'CETA procurement regulation' (4 July 2017) <http://
international.gc.ca/trade-commerce/trade-agreements-accords-commerciaux/
agr-acc/ceta-aecg/text-texte/19.aspx?lang=eng> accessed 6 July 2018

18 European Commission, Trade, Joint Report on the EU-Canada Scoping Exercise
(March 5 2009), <http://trade.ec.europa.eu/doclib/docs/2009/march/tradoc_142470.
pdf> accessed 6 July 2018

19 Government of Canada, Text of the Comprehensive Economic and Trade
Agreement – Chapter nineteen: Government procurement, Article 19.4 – General
Principles, Non-discrimination <http://international.gc.ca/trade-commerce/trade-
agreements-accords-commerciaux/agr-acc/ceta-aecg/text-texte/19.aspx?lang=
eng> accessed 6 July 2018

There has been extensive political commentary about the likelihood of the UK having a trade agreement which is similar to CETA; if this were to happen UK procurement regulation would change. Article 19 of CETA appears to cover many procurement concepts which will be familiar from the EU procurement directives to EU member states. However, although the concepts are familiar, there appears to be less detail in the legislation, for example, there is no provision made for pre-contractual remedies.

WTO[20]-GPA model

GPA trade arrangements

Certain WTO members are party to the Agreement on GPA[21], which regulates the basis on which members give access to their markets. The GPA's fundamental aim is to mutually open government procurement markets among its parties. Broadly speaking, there are two main agreements, the General Agreement on Tariffs and Trade ("GATT") and the General Agreement on Trade in Services ("GATS").

There are approximately 30 agreements and schedules made by individual members in specific areas, such as lower customs duty rates. The set of agreements operate to create non-discriminatory trade arrangements.

GPA and its impact on UK procurement

The GPA is a plurilateral agreement[22] which has previously been used as a starting point for the design of procurement regimes in a number of non-EU countries (the procurement law section text in CETA bears

---

20 The WTO was created in 1995. Prior to this, the General Agreement on Tariffs and Trade (GATT) provided many of the rules for world trade. The GATT agreements (there are now revised versions and updated parts) remains as the WTO's umbrella treaty for trade in goods. In terms of services, there is the General Agreement on Trade in Services (GATS), texts can be found at: <https://www.wto.org/english/docs_e/legal_e/gatt47.pdf> accessed 22 July 2018

21 Protocol Amending the Agreement on Government Procurement, adopted 30 March 2012 (GPA/113)

22 In a WTO context, the term plurilateral agreement reflects that WTO members can choose whether or not to be parties to the agreement. At the time of writing, 19 parties have acceded to the GPA (this covers 47 WTO members, including the EU and its 28 member states, which are covered by the GPA as one party). Ten further WTO members are in the process of acceding to the GPA.

some similarities). It contains less detail than the EU procurement rules, is less formulaic and arguably offers more flexibility.

If the UK were to adopt the GPA regime, there would be some significant differences (particularly the difference in the remedies system and lack of an overarching review body), however the key principles of the GPA would be recognisable to UK contracting authorities and bidders. After a period of readjustment, it is likely that the UK would be able to acclimatise to this regime; by virtue of retaining the PCR 2015 and Concession Contracts Regulations 2016 ("CCR 2016") it should already meet the minimum standards of the GPA regime.

GPA thresholds

If the GPA model were to be adopted, then one particular concern would be how contracts below the GPA thresholds would be governed. Currently each party to the GPA specifies the thresholds above which the GPA applies in its Annexes to Appendix I. The threshold is specified in International Monetary Fund Special Drawing Rights ("SDR") (the unit of account of the "IMF"), and each Party also periodically notifies the national currency equivalent of its thresholds to the WTO.

GPA procedural requirements

Being a party to the GPA and observing its procurement rules does not require continued compliance with EU procurement directives. However, there are certain GPA rules which are relatively detailed and not dissimilar to the existing EU rules. The rules require that open, fair and transparent conditions of competition be ensured in government procurement and there are detailed procedural requirements to this effect. However, whilst the GPA provisions are simpler than the EU procurement rules, many of the cornerstone principles will be familiar when compared to the PCR 2015.

For example, the GPA promotes the use of electronic tools and shorter notice periods when electronic tools are used. There are requirements in relation to avoiding conflicts of interest and preventing corrupt practices. The GPA also includes requirements in relation to the conduct of negotiations[23], minimum deadlines for the prepara-

---

23 Protocol Amending the Agreement on Government Procurement, adopted 30 March 2012 (GPA/113) Article XII, Negotiation

tion and submission of tenders[24], the provision of information about economic and technical requirements, as well as the criteria for awarding the contract, obligations in relation to non-discrimination of technical specifications[25] and fairness.[26] Key differences include the absence of requirements for detailed criteria for the evaluation of bids.

GPA dispute settlement mechanisms

There are requirements regarding the availability and nature of domestic review procedures for supplier challenges, which must be put in place by all parties to the agreement; however, the requirements on challenges and remedies are not as stringent when compared to the PCR 2015[27].

Contracting authorities are given a great deal of discretion on the details of remedies available, when contrasted with the more prescriptive remedies rules contained in the PCR 2015. Article XVIII details domestic review procedures and principles which will be familiar from EU procurement legislation. However, Article XVIII lacks the detail of the EU rules. Concepts such as the standstill period, automatic suspension and the ineffectiveness principle are conspicuous by their absence. In relation to the concept of suspension of the procurement process, which is currently a familiar one in EU public procurement, Article XVIII.9 specifies that parties may adopt procedures which provide for rapid interim measures to preserve the supplier's opportunity to participate in the procurement, including suspension of the procurement process. Compensation may be restricted to costs (with no loss of profit award).

Although automatic suspension is not available under the GPA, suspension may, depending on the implementation of Article XVIII.9, be available if requested. The only explicit obligation which may lead to suspension is that the GPA party shall 'adopt or maintain procedures that provide for rapid interim measures to preserve the supplier's opportunity to participate in the procurement'. There is

---

24 Protocol Amending the Agreement on Government Procurement, adopted 30 March 2012 (GPA/113) Article XI, Time-Periods

25 Protocol Amending the Agreement on Government Procurement, adopted 30 March 2012 (GPA/113) Article X Technical Specifications and Tender Documentation

26 Protocol Amending the Agreement on Government Procurement, adopted 30 March 2012 (GPA/113) Article XV, Treatment of Tenders and Awarding of Contracts.

27 Protocol Amending the Agreement on Government Procurement, adopted 30 March 2012 (GPA/113) Article XVIII, Domestic Review Procedures.

no obligation for the party to choose suspension of the procurement process if there is another rapid interim measure which fulfils the requirement of preserving the supplier's opportunity to participate in the procurement.

It is also worth noting that there is no supranational court for individuals, and the GPA envisages negotiation between states to resolve disputes, which would be a significant change for the UK compared to its current ability to send preliminary references to the CJEU.[28]

Although the GPA contains less detail, it appears to be based on very similar principles to the current EU procurement regime. If the UK were to adopt the GPA approach, it would be possible for contracting authorities and suppliers to adjust to this regime, although it would not be a seamless transition. One downside is that in terms of procurement market access, access to EU procurement markets would be more restricted than it is currently, as the scope of GPA coverage of EU procurement markets is narrower than it is for EU member states. However, there are a number of other countries who are signatories to the GPA, including the US, Japan and Canada. Looking ahead, it is also possible that the GPA may well, over time, evolve in a similar direction to the EU procurement regime.

GPA and UK membership

There was some academic dispute over whether, if the UK were to exit the EU, the UK would need to apply to rejoin the GPA.[29,30] It appears that the UK Government has accepted that currently the UK does not have independent membership and has sought to accede to the GPA.[31]

28 European Commission, DG Internal Market, Industry, Entrepreneurship and SMEs, Economic efficiency and legal effectiveness of review and remedies procedures for public contracts, April 2015 <https://publications.europa.eu/en/publication-detail/-/publication/e07de115-c72a-4bd8-9844-daed732da34f> accessed 22 July 2018

29 Department for International Trade, *Trade White Paper: Preparing for our future UK trade policy, Government Response*, January 2018, <https://assets.publishing.service.gov.uk/government/uploads/system/uploads/attachment_data/file/671953/Trade_White_Paper_response_FINAL.pdf> accessed 28 May 2018

30 ibid 5 <https://assets.publishing.service.gov.uk/government/uploads/system/uploads/attachment_data/file/671953/Trade_White_Paper_response_FINAL.pdf accessed 28/05/2018>

31 Application for accession of the United Kingdom to the Agreement on Government Procurement in its own right <https://docs.wto.org/dol2fe/Pages/FE_Search/FE_S_S009-DP.aspx?Language=E&CatalogueIdList=245666,245668,245669,245670,245671,245719,245701,245667,245658,245655&CurrentCatalogueIdIndex=5&FullTextHash=371857150> accessed 21 July 2018

The UK and the European Commission wrote to the WTO membership in October 2017 on the topic of Brexit, raising the idea of creating a UK-specific Schedule to the WTO Agreement on Government Procurement. The letter mentioned that the EU's current WTO schedules contain commitments which are also applicable to the UK in its capacity as a WTO Member and that from the EU's perspective, these schedules remain applicable to the EU (although there may be some adjustments required in respect of quantitative commitments in the area of goods in light of Brexit). The letter states as follows:

> Following its withdrawal from the EU, the UK will remain a Member of the WTO, subject to all the rights and obligations that this entails. It will have its own separate schedules of commitments for goods and services, to take effect immediately upon leaving the EU. In communicating its own separate schedules before it leaves the EU in March 2019, the UK intends to replicate as far as possible its obligations under the current commitments of the EU.

The letter sets out a roadmap for future arrangements with the WTO. However, it was silent on the need for the UK to go through an accession process to re-join. In June 2018[32], the EU and the UK government wrote a joint letter containing the UK's application to accede to the GPA, stating the following:

> The United Kingdom currently participates in the Government Procurement Agreement by virtue of its membership of the European Union. The United Kingdom has implemented Government Procurement Agreement rules in domestic law for over twenty years, and its government procurement market is one of the most open in the world.
>
> ...
>
> The United Kingdom and the European Union agreed to work together towards the United Kingdom's objective of remaining, in its own right, subject to the rights and obligations it currently has under the Government Procurement Agreement as an European Union Member State on the basis of the commitments which are currently contained in the European Union's schedule.

---

32 ibid.

The UK's position is that by virtue of having implemented EU procurement laws and by retaining them due to the European Union Withdrawal Act ("EUWA"), the UK is compliant with GPA regulatory procurement law requirements. The decision by the UK government to retain the current rights and obligations which it has under the GPA may assist in minimising negotiating time with the WTO over the accession, however at the time of writing there is no final decision on the UK's accession to the GPA, or an agreement between both parties on the exact terms of any accession.

Ukraine's procurement model

Ukraine is due to become closely aligned with the EU's regulatory regime. Ukraine is adopting current and future EU legislation on public procurement and, apart from defence procurement, both the EU and Ukraine will have full access to each other's procurement markets.[33] If the UK were to follow this model, procurement law would remain unchanged. The vast majority of customs duties on goods will be removed as soon as the EU-Ukraine Deep and Comprehensive Free Trade Area ("DCFTA")[34] enters into force. This is a useful illustration of a trade agreement where a third country becomes closely aligned with the EU's regulatory approach and if the UK could accept freedom of movement, this could present a useful model for the UK's future relationship with the EU.

Turkey's procurement model

Another potential trade model is demonstrated by Turkey[35]. Turkey has a customs union agreement[36] with the EU, but the arrangements between Turkey and the EU do not cover all sectors and in particular, do not cover government procurement. In December 2016, the European

---

33 European Commission, *Guide to the EU-Ukraine Deep and Comprehensive Free Trade Area* <https://eeas.europa.eu/sites/eeas/files/tradoc_150981.pdf> accessed 7 May 2018, 5

34 ibid.

35 European Commission, *Trade Policy, Turkey Policies, Information and Services* <http://ec.europa.eu/trade/policy/countries-and-regions/countries/turkey/> accessed 11 June 2018

36 Decision No 1/95 of the EC-Turkey Association Council of 22
    December 1995 on implementing the final phase of the Customs Union (96/142/EC) <https://www.avrupa.info.tr/sites/default/files/2016-09/Custom_Union_des_ENG_0.pdf> accessed 12 June 2018

Commission proposed the modernisation of the arrangements with Turkey, to extend to areas which include public procurement[37], while acknowledging that an ambitious agreement would mean disruptive change for some highly protected Turkish sectors.

The Turkish model is interesting for two reasons. First, it is evidence that it is possible to have a customs union arrangement which does not cover government procurement. This demonstrates that there is potential for UK procurement to not be subject to EU regulation, while the UK still enjoys the benefits of a customs union. Second, it also demonstrates that one of the main difficulties for Turkey, if it were to open up its procurement markets, would be the disruptive process of change. The UK, as its government procurement markets are already aligned with EU requirements, would not need to go through this process of disruption and change in order to align with EU requirements. Therefore, the cost of change would not exist in the same way as it does for Turkey. When considering changing the UK's procurement regime, the deterrent factor is instead focused on policy concerns of loss of border control.

---

37 European Commission, *Study of the EU-Turkey Bilateral Preferential Trade Framework, Including the Customs Union, and an Assessment of Its Possible Enhancement* (Final Report, 26 October 2016), 196–201 <http://trade.ec.europa.eu/doclib/docs/2017/january/tradoc_155240.pdf>, accessed 12 June 2018

6 Favouring national suppliers and the 'Buy British' campaign

Favouring national suppliers will be a contentious topic of debate if procurement law is reformed. EU procurement law currently prevents UK contracting authorities from favouring national suppliers. In cases where a contract being procured appears to have a particular bearing on UK identity, the tension between 'Buy British' sentiments and the non-discrimination principle in EU law is apparent. This tension is illustrated by the judgment in the case of *Harmon*[1], which concerned an expensive fenestration contract for Portcullis House. More recently, the furore over the contract for British passports being awarded to a Franco-Dutch company[2] demonstrates that the opposition between 'Buy British' sentiments and EU non-discrimination principles remains relevant. If procurement law reform is to be the direction of travel, this concern is likely to be near the top of the reform agenda.

Equal treatment of bidders from different member states is one of the key principles of EU procurement law, referenced in the first recital of Directive 2014/24/EU,

> The award of public contracts by or on behalf of Member States' authorities has to comply with the principles of the Treaty on the Functioning of the European Union (TFEU), and in particular the free movement of goods, freedom of establishment and the freedom to provide services, as well as the principles deriving therefrom, such as equal treatment, non-discrimination, mutual recognition, proportionality and transparency.

1 *Harmon CFEM Facades (UK) Ltd v The Corporate Officer of the House of Commons* [1999] All ER (D) 1178
2 OJEU Contract Notice, 2017/S 058-107947, published 1 July 2018, Passport Production and Associated Services. <http://ted.europa.eu/TED/notice/udl?uri=TED:NOTICE:107947-2017:TEXT:EN:HTML&src=0> accessed 12 June 2018

Consequently, one of the key premises of EU public procurement law is that a competition cannot be designed to advantage national suppliers.

The recitals to Directive 2014/24 provide more detail on how this principle should be observed, stating that award criteria, '... should not be chosen or applied in a way that discriminates directly or indirectly against economic operators from other Member States'.

The domestic legislation The Public Services (Social Value) Act 2015 focuses on how a contracting authority can use a procurement process to improve the environmental, social and economic well-being of the area. However, there is no reference in the Procurement Policy Note guidance to how the domestic legislation interacts with the obligations set out in EU Treaty principles or in the procurement directives.

Recital 92 of Directive 2014/24[3] states that any criteria set should be 'linked to the subject-matter of the contract', which includes award criteria including environmental and social aspects. Therefore, EU law imposes stricter requirements in relation to environmental, social and economic considerations than domestic law does. As EU law takes precedence over domestic legislation, currently the UK must observe EU legislation in this respect, as demonstrated in the well-known case of *Harmon*[4].

Case study: Buying British: Harmon

The case of *Harmon* illustrates the significance of the principle of non-discrimination on grounds of nationality. This case related to a substantial contract for fenestration work for Portcullis House[5] which was procured using the restricted procedure. The bidder Harmon submitted the lowest price bid, and the contract was awarded to the bidder Seele/Alvis. Harmon had various grounds of complaint, including that Seele/Alvis had been given preferential treatment on the grounds of nationality.

The court concluded that the winning bidder, Seele/Alvis, a UK company, which had both UK and German involvement, had been given preference in the procurement process due to its UK connections. Specifically, the judge concluded that Seele/Alvis had been given preferential treatment by being both invited to bid and in being encouraged to submit the alternative bid which was eventually selected as the winning bid; 'the defendant ... applied arbitrary methods to favour Seele Alvis' tender at the expense of Harmon'.[6] It appears from

---

3 Directive 2014/24/EU, Recital 92
4 *Harmon* (n 86)
5 Portcullis House provides office space for MPs
6 ibid [205]

the procurement case that partly because of the national significance of Portcullis House, there was some motivation to breach the procurement law principles and 'Buy British'.[7,8]

This tension, between EU procurement obligations of non-discrimination and the desire to award contracts of symbolic national significance to national suppliers, is also demonstrated in the case study below.

Case study: Buying British: Contract Award for manufacture of British passports

Spring 2018 brought controversy over the anticipated award of a contract for the manufacture of new British passports to Gemalto, a Franco-Dutch company.[9] It provides a useful illustration of the difficulties that will be faced if the prevailing political preference is to give precedence to 'buy British' sentiments over and above procurement obligations. The Official Journal of the European Union ("OJEU") contract notice[10] for this particular procurement was published in March 2017. It indicates that the procurement was run under the Competitive Procedure with Negotiation, price was not the only award criterion and the contract value was estimated to be £490,000,000. The incumbent supplier, De La Rue is headquartered in England and also tendered in the competition. It has been reported in the news[11] that Gemalto's offer was significantly cheaper (approximately £50,000,000) than the incumbent supplier's offer. The Home office blog post on this issue states that 'the preferred bid will save the taxpayer approximately £120 million during the lifetime of the new contract', although it is not clear how

---

7 It should be noted that there are some exceptions relating to defence and national security contracts.

8 It was deemed to be a breach of Article 6 of the EC Treaty, now Article 18 of the Treaty on the Functioning of the European Union (TFEU) https://eur-lex.europa. eu/legal-content/EN/TXT/?uri=CELEX:12012E/TXT accessed 22 July 2018

9 Financial Times: Opinion, Blue passports and public procurement, Why Brexit may mean more public contracts going to foreign companies, David Allen Green https://www.ft.com/content/7fcd730e-2ddd-11e8-9b4b-bc4b9f08f381 accessed 30 March 2018

10 OJEU Contract Notice, 2017/S 058-107947, published 23/3/17, Passport Production and Associated Services <http://ted.europa.eu/TED/notice/udl?uri=TED: NOTICE:107947-2017:TEXT:EN:HTML&src=0> accessed 22 July 2018

11 Brexit: Leavers in uproar over 'national humiliation' as blue passports contract 'handed to Franco-Dutch firm', The Independent, 22 March 2018 <https://www. independent.co.uk/news/uk/politics/brexit-latest-blue-british-passports-contract-gemalto-national-humiliation-eu-exit-france-a8267761.html> accessed 22 July 2018

this saving has been calculated.[12] The anticipated contract award decision has caused a public outcry[13], blue passports and their national production being seen as symbolic of British identity. However, as at the time of writing, the UK is still bound by EU procurement rules and, as discussed above, discrimination on the grounds of nationality of the tenderer is not permitted. Therefore, the most economically advantageous tender, selected through an EU procurement process, is due to be awarded the contract, to commence in 2019. Consequently, British passports will be produced by Gemalto, headquartered in Amsterdam.

Under current EU procurement rules, the number of options to ensure that passports were produced by a British supplier is extremely limited, the only realistic alternative to an EU procurement process being that the passports are produced in-house by a contracting authority, meaning that their production would not fall within the definition of a services contract which would be caught by the EU public procurement rules.

The ability for contracting authorities to 'buy British' after the end of the Transition Period largely depends on the eventual direction of procurement law in any trade agreement reached. However, there is an absence of likely trading models which permit contracting authorities to favour national suppliers. For example, if the UK were to reapply to join the World Trade Organisation's ("WTO") Government Procurement Agreement ("GPA"), they are unlikely to be able to accede with provisions which offer benefit to national suppliers. Therefore, controversies such as the one discussed above are likely to continue.

Case study: Buy Australian: Australia's accession to the GPA

It is unlikely that the UK will be able to 'buy national', as demonstrated by events during Australia's accession to the GPA. The Delegation of the European Union to Australia identified drafting in Australia's procurement rules which arguably favoured Australian suppliers. Article 10.30 required commonwealth officials to consider the economic benefit to the procurement to the Australian economy.[14] The letter raises

---

12 Home Office statement on passport contract, Home Office blog, 22 March 2018, <https://homeofficemedia.blog.gov.uk/2018/03/22/home-office-statement-on-passport-contract/> accessed 22 July 2018

13 The Independent (n 96)

14 Commonwealth (of Australia) Procurement Rules, (Section 105B (1) of the Public Governance, Performance and Accountability Act 2013), <https://www.finance.gov.au/sites/default/files/commonwealth-procurement-rules.pdf> accessed 31 March 2018

concerns that this test of economic benefit to the Australian economy could be applied in a discriminatory manner towards EU suppliers.[15]

Having analysed the procurement rules and associated guidance, the letter refers to Article IV (1) of the GPA[16], which contains a general requirement for non-discrimination. It concludes that the requirement for economic benefit to the Australian economy breaches this general requirement for non-discrimination, requesting that Australia re-examines the provisions to align them with the principles of the GPA.

In conclusion, if the UK agrees a trading arrangement where it either retains compliance or aligns with EU procurement rules, then UK contracting authorities will be unable to 'buy British'. However, even if the UK's trading relationship with the EU becomes more remote and it instead seeks to accede to the GPA in its own right, it is extremely unlikely to be able to discriminate in favour of national suppliers, as demonstrated by the concerns raised in respect of the 'buy Australian' provisions.

Article IV(1) (General Principles) of the GPA demonstrates that the principle of non-discrimination against foreign suppliers is a cornerstone principle of the GPA. It states that parties (and their procuring authorities) to the agreement must treat the products, services and suppliers of any other party no less favourably than they treat local suppliers, or any other party to the agreement. Additionally, parties to the agreement shall not treat domestic suppliers differently due to any foreign affiliation or ownership, or treat any domestic supplier differently due to their goods or services being produced in the territory of another Party. Therefore, if the UK wishes to be able to 'buy British' for public sector contracts, it will not be able to favour domestic parties, meaning that membership of the GPA will not suit its aims.

Buying British: The Equality Act 2010

If revisions were made to domestic procurement law to offer advantages to domestic suppliers, it is probable that the Equality Act 2010 will protect suppliers (in particular employees staffing service contracts), from discrimination on the grounds of nationality. It is arguable that the selection of organisations on the grounds of the nationality or nationalities of that organisation's staff would fall within the definition of direct

---

15 Inquiry into the Commonwealth Procurement Framework Submission 3, European Union Delegation to Australia, Canberra, 24 March 2017 <http://www.aph.gov.au/DocumentStore.ashx?id=759dc14f-835b-42bd-a11e-a2c2e349eca8&subId=509292> accessed 15 July 2018

16 Protocol Amending the Agreement on Government Procurement, adopted 30 March 2012 (GPA/113)

discrimination. Section 9 of the Equality Act 2010[17] states that race includes (a) colour, (b) nationality and (c) ethnic or national origins.

The UK will be entitled to amend the Equality Act after Brexit unless otherwise agreed in negotiations with the EU. However, as the Equality Act 2010 brought together many existing pieces of domestic, as well as EU legislation[18], the UK would need to spend some time considering suitable amendments. To permit discrimination on the grounds of nationality, the UK would also need to consider its obligation under the European Convention on Human Rights.

Artificial narrowing of technical specifications to favour national suppliers

One key principle of procurement law is that the specification should not be artificially narrowed.

Article 42(2) of Directive 2014/24 states, 'Technical specifications shall afford equal access of economic operators to the procurement procedure and shall not have the effect of creating unjustified obstacles to the opening up of public procurement to competition.' Recital 74 states, 'technical specifications should be drafted in such a way as to avoid artificially narrowing down competition through requirements that favour a specific economic operator by mirroring key characteristics of the supplies, services or works habitually offered by that economic operator. Drawing up the technical specifications in terms of functional and performance requirements generally allows that objective to be achieved in the best way possible.'

These rules, which are part of the EU legislative procurement package, will to some extent remain part of UK domestic law on Exit Day. Although the explanatory text from the Recitals will not be incorporated into UK domestic law, the Articles from Directive 2014/24 will remain part of UK law on Exit Day by operation of the European Union Withdrawal Act ("EUWA").[19] Therefore, in line with Regulation 42(1) the starting point is that technical specifications will be constructed so that suppliers have equal access to the procurement

---

17 Equality Act 2010

18 Protecting Human Rights in the UK, The Conservative's Proposals for changing Britain's Human Rights Laws <https://www.conservatives.com/~/media/files/downloadable%20files/human_rights.pdf> accessed 15 July 2018

19 While the recitals to Directive 2015/24/EU have not been transposed into UK law, Article 42(2) has been transposed into Regulation 42(10) and this requirement will therefore be "saved" within UK law on exit day by the European Union (Withdrawal) Act.

process. This approach maximises the likelihood that competition will be on a level playing field and suppliers will not be disadvantaged by a technical specification which is unduly narrow and therefore favours one particular supplier over another. Regulation 42 will be saved within domestic law, but amenable to modification or amendment. The UK may allow narrow specifications which might favour certain product manufacturers or might favour national suppliers.

EU view on discriminatory procurement policies

The EU's recent Communication on making public procurement work for Europe[20] identified that currently some of the EU's trade partners follow discriminatory practices in favour of national suppliers. The EU's Communication is clear on its position in respect of these activities, observing the following:

> The EU is the world's most open market for procurement, but access for our companies in other countries is not always reciprocal. Major EU trade partners maintain discriminatory measures affecting EU businesses by granting preferential treatment to national bidders. The Commission's reflection paper on harnessing globalisation stressed that restoring a level playing field is more than ever necessary and called for a rapid adoption of an international procurement instrument. This would increase the European Union's leverage in its negotiations with trade partners. There is an urgent need to unlock the current stalemate in the Council with regard to this instrument.

The footnote in the Communication refers to the policies 'Buy American', 'Make in India' and 'Buy Chinese' as examples of discriminatory procurement policies. Therefore, the EU's view on trade partners who maintain pro-national procurement procedures is clear. Its intention to ensure that if a trade partner closes its procurement markets to the EU, that the EU takes action in response. The international procurement instrument referred to elsewhere in the book demonstrates this.

---

20 European Commission, Communication from the Commission to the European Parliament, the Council, the European Economic and Social Committee and the Committee of the Regions, Making Public Procurement work in and for Europe, Strasbourg, 3.10.2017 <https://eur-lex.europa.eu/legal-content/EN/TXT/?uri=COM%3A2017%3A572%3AFIN> accessed 15 July 2018

7   Potential revisions of the procurement regime

Potential revisions of the procurement regime – simplifying the current procurement system

UK procurement is an outlier among EU Member States[1]; the UK is the only Member State in which the open procedure is not the most frequently used. Instead, the UK often uses the restricted procedure, a practice which is in decline in other Member States. The reasons for use of the restricted procedure include the perception that it reduces the cost of evaluating bids, as the number of applicants who proceed to the tender stage are fewer. There is also a view that as there are fewer tenderers competing at tender stage in the restricted procedure, this is more attractive to tenderers, as it increases the probability of contract award. The counter-arguments are that restricted procurement procedures are lengthier than open procedures and that tender stage questions are often more complex and require additional resource from both tenderers and contracting authorities to complete and evaluate.

Public procurement procedures are time and resource intensive. The 2011 Commission report analysed the time taken for different types of procurement procedures. This report recorded that the average time

---

1 Directorate-General for Regional and Urban Policy (European Commission) 'Stock-taking of administrative capacity, systems and practices across the EU to ensure the compliance and quality of public procurement involving European Structural and Investment (ESI) Funds' [13 April 2016] <https://publications.europa. eu/en/publication-detail/-/publication/d1082259-0202-11e6-b713-01aa75ed71a1> accessed 1 July 2018

Directorate-General for Regional and Urban Policy (European Commission) 'Public procurement – Study on administrative capacity in the EU, United Kingdom Country Profile' [13 April 2016] <http://ec.europa.eu/regional_policy/sources/policy/how/improving-investment/public-procurement/study/country_profile/uk.pdf> accessed 1 July 2018

necessary to award a contract was around 58 days. The time taken ranged from 45 days for simpler contracts, to up to 245 days for more complex contracts, such as those procured under the competitive dialogue procedure.

Public procurement procedures are put in place to support and manage public resources. Any public procurement procedure needs to balance observing procedural requirements such as transparency, equal treatment, objectivity and clear and non-discriminatory specifications against the need for efficient, flexible, low-cost procedures. It may be possible to rethink some elements of the current procurement procedures on offer or change their appeal, for example, the open procedure could be used more frequently than it currently is.

One opportunity that Brexit could present is the simplification of procurement processes. Any changes would need to balance the preference for simplicity, affordability and ease of process with the need for sufficiently robust selection and award procedures. However, it is possible that a divergence from EU procurement procedures could open up the possibility for the UK to look to streamline its procurement practices. One option could be through greater use of the open procedure, as modelled by other EU member states. Alternatively, a more radical reform could be considered; the UK could look to remodel procurement procedures. It could introduce a more flexible procurement regime based only on key, recognisable principles (such as transparency, equal treatment, etc.). This would remove the necessity for specific procurement procedures to be prescribed and followed. There is some precedent for this in the Concession Contracts Regulations 2016 ("CCR 2016"). The CCR 2016 contains the concept of procedural guarantees which are required to be observed regardless of the exact format of the procurement process followed. This could allow authorities to choose the elements of procurement procedures which best suit their timeframes and the complexity of the contract they are procuring.

Potential revisions of the procurement regime – below threshold contracts

If the UK is looking to construct its own public procurement regime, then it has a number of options for how to approach the question of below threshold contracts, depending on its policy preferences and the requirements of any trade agreements which it may become party to.

If the UK were to design its own procurement policy then it would need to consider the question of thresholds. It could prescribe a threshold above which contracts are regulated and subject to competition and below which they are not regulated. Currently, below threshold contracts are excluded from the application of the procurement directives; however, EU public procurement case law means that in situations where there may be cross-border interest in a contract, a sub-threshold contract should be advertised across the EU and a competitive process should be run. EU case law how to assess cross-border interest is reasonably stringent, with the case of *Mansfield*[2] pointing out that the authority needs to carry out extensive due diligence to satisfy itself regarding whether or not there is cross-border interest in a contract. Contracting authorities need to consider whether a supplier from another Member State would be interested, for example, due to the subject matter of the contract, the value of the contract, the nature of the market or the geographical location of the place of performance. The authority has to record details as to why its approach is justified and the steps taken to identify whether suppliers might be interested. If there is cross-border interest, an advertised competitive process complying with the principles of transparency, impartiality, non-discrimination and equal treatment should be held. Therefore, there is a reasonably substantial obligation placed on contracting authorities.

The UK may choose to remove this obligation to consider cross-border interest altogether if it does not agree a deal with the EU which requires the opening of its public procurement markets. It may also look to vary or remove any financial thresholds above which contracts need to be advertised. Another option would be for the UK to define 'tiers' of financial thresholds, for example, contracts above a certain amount must be advertised locally. Contracts above a certain (higher) amount must be advertised nationally. Another option is that certain sectors could require contract advertisement, while other sectors are excluded or only require advertisement at a higher financial threshold. While these proposals might be seen as increasing the complexity of procurement rules, the concepts of differing threshold levels for differing contract classifications does exist already in the current EU procurement law structure.

Potential revisions of the procurement regime – remedies regime after Brexit

There are various options for the administrative application of the remedies regime after Brexit. It could remain unchanged. Other options include a court-based system similar to the current system,

---

2 *Mansfield District Council v Secretary of State for Communities and Local Government* [2014] EWHC 2167

but with some amendments to allow for a fast-track process and a reduction in costs. Alternatively, there could be a new approach where complex cases remain in the court system, and there is a tribunal system for certain types of cases. An entirely tribunal-based system is also a possibility, as is a system which is based on judicial review of procurement law decisions.

Remedies regime after Brexit – fast-track or tribunal process

A fast-track process, whether in the court system or in a separate tribunal system, would offer some advantages. The criteria for a claim to proceed through the fast-track process would need to be carefully designed, they could include factors such as the value of the contract, the types of remedies being sought and the complexity of the legal issues at hand.

One downside of a court-based system is that SMEs[3] may well find it hard to access the system, due to court fees that are likely to be higher than tribunal-based approaches. A fast-track process could reduce the fees paid by applicants, as the burden on court resources will be reduced. Alternatively, fast-track cases could be heard by a tribunal. However, it would be important that the procedural rights afforded to participants using a fast-track process are not compromised in favour of efficiency.

An option which could be considered is for all parties to bear their own costs in a tribunal system. This could be more onerous for SMEs; in this situation even if a bidder's claim is successful it would not receive any payment of the tribunal or legal costs incurred. It would have spent money on costs which it would not be compensated for, simply by virtue of being the unfortunate recipient of a public procurement error. Nonetheless, if the tribunal system costs were modest, this could be a model which offers the advantage of speed and accessibility.

Remedies regime after Brexit – Shorter and Flexible Trials pilot scheme

At the time of writing there is a Shorter and Flexible Trials pilot scheme running.[4] While this has not currently been deemed suitable for public

---

3 Small and medium-sized enterprises
4 Courts and Tribunals Judiciary, Shorter and Flexible Trial Procedure Guide, <https://www.judiciary.gov.uk/wp-content/uploads/2015/09/Shorter-and-Flexible-Trial-Schemes-Announcement.pdf> accessed 11 August 2018

procurement cases, the principles behind this scheme may offer ideas which could influence a potential model for public procurement cases.

The Shorter and Flexible Trial Procedure Guide states the following:

> The aim of both pilot schemes is to achieve shorter and earlier trials for business related litigation, at a reasonable and proportionate cost. The procedures should also help to foster a change in litigation culture, which involves recognition that comprehensive disclosure and a full, oral trial on all issues is often not necessary for justice to be achieved. That recognition will in turn lead to significant savings in the time and costs of litigation[5].

If a similar approach could be taken to procurement cases then this could expedite trials which have relatively straightforward issues so that cases could reach a quicker and more cost-effective resolution.

Remedies regime after Brexit – remedies review

It could also be possible to review the remedies on offer. For example, one alternative is to stop the automatic suspension entirely and only allow interim contracts to be awarded during a dispute.

Another option, which may be somewhat controversial, is that damages could be removed from the remedies option. Other remedies, such as the requirement to set aside a decision, or potentially the requirement to rewind or re-run the procurement process, could remain. There is a case to be made, that, as a matter of policy, public authorities should not be paying damages. While it is important for there to be dissuasive remedies in place to protect against public procurement breaches, it can be argued that taxpayers' money should not be used to compensate private businesses for loss suffered. The counter argument is of course that accountability is important for an effective public procurement regime. While alternatives such as these might generate some debate, there are a range of options which could be considered as part of a re-design of the public procurement process.

Remedies regime after Brexit – remedies systems in other EU member states

Remedies systems in other EU member states are often more efficient. The European Commission report on the effectiveness of the remedies

5 ibid.

regime reports that at the time the review was carried out, fourteen countries had administrative public procurement review bodies.[6] In the remaining member states, an existing judicial review body is responsible for the review of procurement procedures.

The report detailed that in countries where there are administrative public procurement review bodies, these tend to be more effective. A total of 77.7% respondents to the public consultation gave the view that public procurement procedures before ordinary courts take a longer period of time and also the adjudication outcomes are of a lower standard when compared to specialised administrative review bodies.[7]

The review found that although the costs of review procedures vary across member states, the consultation did not conclude that these costs were dissuasive when considering access to remedies. This would appear to suggest, based on the responses to the consultation, that complainants will still access the remedies system despite cost considerations. The key remaining factor is therefore the speed at which the process takes place.

Remedies regime after Brexit – equality

If the remedies regime were to be altered then a decision would need to be made in respect of whether any alterations would apply to both domestic bidders and third-party country bidders. The UK may wish to give advantages to its own bidders by offering a full range of remedies in the event of a successful procurement complaint. For example, ineffectiveness may not be available to bidders from a third-party country. However, it would still remain available to domestic bidders. The policy reasoning behind this could be so that domestic suppliers are encouraged to bid in UK procurement processes, on the basis that they will enjoy access to a full range of rights in the event of a dispute. Alternatively, depending on the policy direction of the UK and the

---

6 Bulgaria, Cyprus, the Czech Republic, Germany, Denmark, Estonia, Spain, Croatia, Hungary, Malta, Poland, Romania, Slovenia, Slovakia. Report from the Commission to the European parliament and the Council on the effectiveness of Directive 89/665/EEC and Directive 92/13/EEC, as modified by Directive 2007/66/EC, concerning review procedures in the area of public procurement (24.1.17) <http://eur-lex.europa.eu/legal-content/EN/TXT/?uri=COM:2017:28:FIN> accessed 4 May 2018 It should also be noted that this report is based on Directives 89/665/EEC and 92/13/EEC, as amended through Directive 2007/66/EC

7 ibid para 3

degree to which the UK wishes to encourage cross-border trade, this may not be seen to be an approach that will help cross-border trade, as suppliers from third-party countries will be discouraged from bidding in UK procurement processes on the basis that they will not have effective redress in the event of a complaint. This would be less problematic for larger multinational suppliers who may well have a base in the UK which they can use as a bidding entity and will therefore be able to access the remedies available to UK suppliers.

8 The future of procurement law

Procurement law during the Transition Period

Predicting the shape of procurement law during the Transition Period is a relatively straightforward exercise; Title VIII of the European Commission Draft Withdrawal Agreement ("DWA") contains rules determining how to identify contracts which will continue to be subject to the EU procurement regime after the expiry of the Transition Period. Admittedly, not all of the procurement issues which are likely to arise are addressed, for example, there are no explicit provisions in relation to the modification of contracts, however it provides an overall structure for procurement law which appears largely coherent.

The more significant issue is how to predict the direction which UK procurement law will take after the end of the Transition Period. As matters stand it is difficult to predict the shape of procurement law after this point; its trajectory is inseparable from the trade arrangements which are due to be concluded by the EU and UK. Clues about procurement law's potential future can be gleaned from the UK government's policy statements in respect of the preferred UK-EU relationship, from their policy statements in respect of how to approach regulatory areas such as competition law and state aid and from the limited information available about steps which the UK government is taking to liaise with the World Trade Organisation ("WTO").

Procurement law after the Transition Period

The UK and the EU are starting from a place of an identical procurement law regulatory regime, regulated by the same EU Directives in relation to public contracts and concession contracts. After the transposition of Directive 2014/24 into the Public Contracts Regulations 2015 ("PCR 2015"), some miscellaneous obligations were added in

Part 4 of the PCR 2015.[1] However, as the Part 4 obligations are domestic additions, the procurement regime which the UK is currently operating contains the same minimum regulatory standards as every other EU member state's procurement regime (if the EU Directives have been transposed correctly in those member states).

As the UK and EU are starting from a place of complete harmonisation in terms of procurement law, this is a situation for which there is no precedent, as other trade agreements (or new EU member states) would have begun at a place of regulatory divergence and worked towards alignment of procurement rules. It is likely, depending on the solution chosen, that regulatory divergence will incur additional costs, whether it is the costs of determining, drafting, adopting and implementing new legislation, or the more easily quantifiable costs of tariffs and customs duties.

If the UK decides that its procurement law regime should diverge from the EU, this process will break new ground and presents an opportunity to shape what is currently a tightly regulated procurement regime.

Title VIII of the DWA appears to be premised on the UK leaving the EU without any arrangements in place to maintain the existing procurement regulatory framework after the end of the Transition Period. This would arguably be a worst-case outcome. It could occur either if the UK were to leave the EU without a mutually agreed trade deal (i.e. a 'cliff-edge' scenario), or if trade arrangements were agreed but procurement regulation was not included in the scope of the agreement. In this situation, the UK's procurement law would continue to be based on the PCR 2015 and Concession Contracts Regulations 2016 ("CCR 2016") and the existing body of UK procurement case law. Access to eCertis would terminate during the final quarter of 2021. If no arrangement was made with the EU in relation to Court of Justice of the European Union ("CJEU") jurisdiction, then it is unlikely that the UK would be able to make preliminary references to the CJEU to provide interpretations of points of EU law in relation to the PCR 2015 and CCR 2016. The UK would not have a formal mechanism for applying EU procurement case law principles to UK procurement practice. The lack of access to eCertis, inability to seek preliminary rulings and take account of relevant EU case law would prevent UK procurement regulation from keeping pace with EU procurement rules.

---

1 These obligations in Part 4 largely concern domestic advertising through Contracts Finder, and obligations in relation to the payment of invoices.

This in itself would not immediately prevent UK bidders from bidding in EU procurement markets and vice versa.

However, EU procurement law evolves through the gradual development of case law principles, as well as legislative reform. It is almost inevitable that there will be a point at which UK procurement law will fail to keep pace with EU procurement law and that EU bidders may be of the view that they are consequently being disadvantaged. Once this occurs, the pending International Procurement Instrument is likely to mean that UK bidders will be significantly disadvantaged in EU procurement processes, unless the UK's application to accede to the Government Procurement Agreement ("GPA") is successful and the EU and the UK offer procurement market reciprocity to one another.

Probable direction of procurement law

There are a number of arguments why the UK should reform procurement law. For example, the complexity of the procurement rules can lead to confusion over their correct application and the need for frequent legal advice. Running a procurement process is often a costly and time-consuming exercise. Another argument that can be made is the inability to offer local suppliers advantageous access to contracts and the inability to offer local labour opportunities. Theoretically the UK could look to amend procurement law to commence at the end of the Transition Period.

However, the counterweight to many of the reasons for reform, such as the desire to buy British, or to minimise regulatory burdens on contracting authorities, is that if the UK wishes to maintain trading relationships, these trading relationships will almost undoubtedly require reciprocal market access. Consequently, the likelihood that buying British will be permitted is low. Regulatory burdens on contracting authorities, for example around debriefing of bidders, are likely to still be required in the interests of transparency.

Repealing the current procurement legislation would not free the UK from the main tenets of EU procurement law which it objects to. It would instead remove what is arguably a well-honed system which, although cumbersome at points, nonetheless is prescriptive enough to provide guidance on specific areas of confusion as to how to comply with the rules around the use of fair trade labels, or lifecycle costing, which are specific areas of concern emanating from the fundamental principles of transparency, equal treatment and procedural fairness.

Part II

Key Legislation and Recommended Reading

9 Annex
Summary Dashboard

Table 9.1 Impact of Brexit on UK Procurement Law

	Matters staying the same	*Minor issues to iron out*	*Major issues needing urgent political or legislative resolution*
Hard Brexit ("no deal" exit)	PCR 2015 and CCR 2016 will remain on the UK statute books – amendments may need to be made to these depending on the terms of the deal.	If the GPA application is still in negotiation, the GPA may have some queries about the UK's coverage and commitments	Agreement with other countries and trade partners as to the coverage of procurement markets. Solutions may include: • Accession to the GPA • Bespoke bilateral or plurilateral agreements agreeing coverage, procurement principles and remedies regimes
	The UK's application to accede to the GPA has already been submitted and negotiations can continue, or the UK's application may be accepted	The majority of the issues to be resolved will be major issues.	

(*Continued*)

	Matters staying the same	*Minor issues to iron out*	*Major issues needing urgent political or legislative resolution*
Bespoke trade deal	PCR 2015 and CCR 2016 will remain on the UK statute books – amendments may need to be made to these depending on the terms of the deal. The UK's application to accede to the GPA has already been submitted and negotiations can continue, or the UK's application may be accepted	Access to: • eCertis • OJEU Tenders Electronic Daily advertising system	• Accession to the GPA • Trade agreement which covers public procurement markets • Details of the extent of procurement market coverage • Remedies regime • Administrative body to adjudicate on remedies regime • Depending on the agreement with the EU, the UK may be required to align with EU procurement law
Soft Brexit (remaining in the single market or EEA)	Depending on the date of agreement, the provisions of the EUWA disapplying the ECA 1972 may either be repealed or not take effect. EU procurement directives and CJEU case law are most likely to will continue to apply to the UK Access to eCertis and the OJEU Tenders Electronic Daily advertising system will continue.	Remedies administrative regime, which could be any of: • CJEU • EFTA court • A new tribunal system	Whether the UK remains able to influence the future development of EU procurement law (unlikely if a Norway-style deal is agreed)

Abbreviation list

CCR 2016	Concession Contracts Regulations 2016
CJEU	Court of Justice of the European Union
ECA 1972	European Communities Act 1972
eCertis	a tool used to identify and compare certificates requested in public procurement procedures across the EU
EEA	European Economic Area
EFTA	European Free Trade Association
EUWA	European Union (Withdrawal) Act
GPA	Government Procurement Agreement
PCR 2015	Public Contracts Regulations 2015 (as amended)
OJEU	Official Journal of the European Union

10 Key pieces of legislation

Table A.1 Summary of Whether Key Legislation May Be Amended or Repealed Due to Brexit

Legislation	Commentary and analysis; will this legislation be amended or repealed due to Brexit?
Public Contracts Regulations 2015 (as amended)	Retained by the UK. Depending on the trade deal and procurement provisions agreed, some amendments may be made, for example, references to owing the same duties to EEA suppliers as to UK suppliers, or references to the status of the ESPD document.
Concession Contracts Regulations 2016	Retained by the UK. Minimal, or no amendments to be made.
Directive 2014/24/ EU on public procurement	Retained by the EU Some small changes will be needed, for example Directive 2014/24 details the UK's central government authorities. This is likely to be amended. Similarly, Annex XI refers to how to obtain verification in the UK of entries on professional or trade registers and this is likely to be removed.
Directive 2014/23/ EU on the award of concession contracts	Retained by the EU There are unlikely to be any specific amendments required to account for the UK's departure, or minimal amendments.

Abbreviation list

EEA   European Economic Area
ESPD   European Single Procurement Document

11 Recommended reading
Bibliography

Primary sources

Cases

UK cases

Harmon CFEM Facades (UK) Ltd v The Corporate Officer of the House of Commons [1999] All ER (D) 1178

Mansfield District Council v Secretary of State for Communities and Local Government [2014] EWHC 2167

EU cases

Case C-324/98 *Telaustria and Telefonadress* [2000] ECR I-10745

Other jurisdictions

Casino Admiral AG v Wolfgang Egger [2014] E-24/13 <http://www.eftacourt.int/fileadmin/user_upload/Files/Cases/2013/24_13/24_13_Judgment_EN.pdf> accessed 11 June 2018

Legislation

UK legislation - primary

Equality Act 2010
The European Communities Act 1972
European Union (Withdrawal) Act 2018, Section 2(1)

UK legislation - secondary

Concession Contracts Regulations 2016 (SI 2016/273) < Public Contract Regulations 2015 (SI 2015/102), (as amended)

EU legislation - primary

Treaty on the Functioning of the European Union (Consolidated version), OJ C 326, 26.10.2012,

EU legislation - secondary

Commission Implementing Regulation (EU) 2016/7 of 5 January 2016 establishing the standard form for the European Single Procurement Document (Text with EEA relevance), OJ L 3, 6.1.2016, pp. 16–34

Commission Regulation (EU) 2017/2367of 18 December 2017amending Directive 2009/81/EC of the European Parliament and of the Council in respect of the application thresholds for the procedures for the award of contracts (Text with EEA relevance)

Commission Regulation (EC) No 213/2008 of 28 November 2007 amending Regulation (EC) No 2195/2002 of the European Parliament and of the Council on the Common Procurement Vocabulary (CPV) and Directives 2004/17/EC and 2004/18/EC of the European Parliament and of the Council on public procurement procedures, as regards the revision of the CPV (Text with EEA relevance)

Directive 2014/23/EU of the European Parliament and of the Council of 26 February 2014 on the award of concession contracts (Text with EEA relevance), OJ L 94, 28.3.2014, pp. 1–64

Directive 2014/24/EU of the European Parliament and of the Council of 26 February 2014 on public procurement and repealing Directive 2004/18/EC (Text with EEA relevance), OJ L 94, 28.3.2014, pp. 65–242

Directive 2014/25/EU of the European Parliament and of the Council of 26 February 2014 on procurement by entities operating in the water, energy, transport and postal services sectors and repealing Directive 2004/17/EC (Text with EEA relevance), OJ L 94, 28.3.2014, pp. 243–374

Other jurisdictions

Agreement on the European Economic Area [2016] OJ No L 1, <http://www.efta.int/media/documents/legal-texts/eea/the-eea-agreement/Main%20Text%20of%20the%20Agreement/EEAagreement.pdf> accessed 11 June 2018

Agreement between the European Community and the Swiss Confederation on certain aspects of government procurement - Final Act - Joint Declarations - Information relating to the entry into force of the seven Agreements with the Swiss Confederation in the sectors free movement of persons, air and land transport, public procurement, scientific and technological cooperation, mutual recognition in relation to conformity assessment, and trade in agricultural products, OJ L 114, 30.4.2002, pp. 430–467 < https://eur-lex.europa.eu/legal-content/EN/TXT/?uri=uriserv:OJ.L_.2002.114.01.0430.01.ENG> accessed 15 June 2018

Commonwealth (of Australia) Procurement Rules, (Section 105B (1) of the Public Governance, Performance and Accountability Act 2013), https://www.finance.gov.au/sites/default/files/commonwealth-procurement-rules.pdf accessed 31 March 2018

Decision No 1/95 of the EC-Turkey Association Council of 22 December 1995 on implementing the final phase of the Customs Union (96/142/EC) <https://www.avrupa.info.tr/sites/default/files/2016-09/Custom_Union_des_ENG_0.pdf> accessed 12 June 2018

EEA Agreement, Annex XVI, Procurement [1 June 2018] <http://www.efta.int/media/documents/legal-texts/eea/the-eea-agreement/Annexes%2520to%2520the%2520Agreement/annex16.pdf> accessed 12 June 2018

Federal Act of Public Procurement of December 16 1994, Switzerland, (as amended) (SR 172.056.1)

Federal Ordinance of Public Procurement of December 11 1995, Switzerland, (SR 172.056.11)

General Agreement on Trade in Services, <https://www.wto.org/english/docs_e/legal_e/gatt47.pdf> accessed 22 July 2018

Government of Canada, 'CETA procurement regulation' (4 July 2017) <http://international.gc.ca/trade-commerce/trade-agreements-accords-commerciaux/agr-acc/ceta-aecg/text-texte/19.aspx?lang=eng> accessed 6 July 2018

Intercantonal Agreement on Public Procurement of November 25 1994/March 15 2001 (Switzerland)

Protocol Amending the Agreement on Government Procurement, adopted 30 March 2012 (GPA/113)

Secondary sources

Baume, M, 'No Brexit transition deal until progress on withdrawal, Guy Verhofstadt says comments from David Davis that agreement is not 'legally enforceable' undermined trust', *Politico*, (1 December 2017) <https://www.politico.eu/article/manfred-weber-guy-verhofstadt-eu-parliament-no-brexit-transition-deal-until-progress-on-withdrawal/> accessed 24 July 2017

The Conservatives, Protecting Human Rights in the UK, The Conservative's Proposals for changing Britain's Human Rights Laws, <https://www.conservatives.com/~/media/files/downloadable%20files/human_rights.pdf> accessed 15 July 2018

Courts and Tribunals Judiciary, Shorter and Flexible Trial Procedure Guide, <https://www.judiciary.gov.uk/wp-content/uploads/2015/09/Shorter-and-Flexible-Trial-Schemes-Announcement.pdf> accessed 11 August 2018

Crown Commercial Service, New Thresholds 2018, Information Note PPN 04/17 December 2017 <https://assets.publishing.service.gov.uk/government/uploads/system/uploads/attachment_data/file/670666/PPN_0417_New_Thresholds_2018__1_.pdf> accessed 11 August 2018

Delegation of the European Union Letter to World Trade Organization Membership containing an application for accession of the United Kingdom to the Agreement on Government Procurement in its own right (1 June 2018) <https://docs.wto.org/dol2fe/Pages/FE_Search/FE_S_S009-DP.aspx? Language=E&CatalogueIdList=245666,245668,245669,245670,245671, 245719,245701,245667,245658,245655&CurrentCatalogueIdIndex=5&Full TextHash=371857150> accessed 21 July 2018

Directorate-General for Regional and Urban Policy (European Commission) 'Stock-taking of administrative capacity, systems and practices across the EU to ensure the compliance and quality of public procurement involving European Structural and Investment (ESI) Funds' (13 April 2016) <https:// publications.europa.eu/en/publication-detail/-/publication/d1082259-0202-11e6-b713-01aa75ed71a1> accessed 1 July 2018

Directorate-General for Regional and Urban Policy (European Commission) 'Public procurement – Study on administrative capacity in the EU, United Kingdom Country Profile' (13 April 2016) <http://ec.europa.eu/regional_ policy/sources/policy/how/improving-investment/public-procurement/ study/country_profile/uk.pdf> accessed 1 July 2018

European Commission, *Task Force for the Preparation and Conduct of the Negotiations with the United Kingdom under Article 50 TEU, Draft Agreement on the withdrawal of the United Kingdom of Great Britain and Northern Ireland from the European Union and the European Atomic Energy Community,* (19 March 2018), 1 <https://ec.europa.eu/commission/sites/beta-political/files/draft_agreement_coloured.pdf> accessed 9 May 2018

European Commission, *Position paper on On-going Public Procurement Procedures, European Commission to UK,* (TF50 (2017) 12/2 20 September 2017), <https://ec.europa.eu/commission/sites/beta-political/files/public_ procurement.pdf> accessed 24 July 2017

European Commission, *Communication to the European Parliament, the Council, the European Economic and Social Committee and the Committee of the Regions, Making Public Procurement work in and for Europe,* Strasbourg, (3.10.2017), COM(2017) 572 final, <http://eur-lex.europa.eu/legal-content/EN/ TXT/PDF/?uri=CELEX:52017DC0572&from=EN> accessed 26 May 2018

European Commission, *Draft Withdrawal Agreement on the withdrawal of the United Kingdom of Great Britain and Northern Ireland from the European Union and the European Atomic Energy Community, (19 March 2018) TF50 (2018) 33 – Commission to EU 27,* <https://ec.europa.eu/commission/sites/ beta-political/files/draft_agreement_coloured.pdf> accessed 9 May 2018

European Commission, 'Single Market and Standards, Common Procurement Vocabulary' <https://ec.europa.eu/growth/single-market/public-procurement/ rules-implementation/common-vocabulary_en> accessed 28 May 2018

European Commission, DG Internal Market and Services, *Final Report, Review of the Functioning of the CPV codes/system,* MARKT/2011/111/C, (December 2012), http://ec.europa.eu/DocsRoom/documents/21583/attachments/1/translations accessed 28 May 2018

European Commission, *Amended proposal for a Regulation of the European Parliament and of the Council on the access of third-country goods and services to the Union's internal market in public procurement and procedures supporting negotiations on access of Union goods and services to the public procurement markets of third countries*, Brussels, (29 January 2016), COM(2016) 34 final, 2012/0060 (COD) <http://trade.ec.europa.eu/doclib/docs/2016/january/tradoc_154187.pdf> accessed 22 July 2018

European Commission, Press release, 'European Commission Takes Action to Open Up International Procurement Markets', Brussels, (29 January 2016) http://europa.eu/rapid/press-release_IP-16-178_en.htm accessed 22 July 2018

European Commission, 'Comprehensive Economic and Trade Agreement in Focus', <http://ec.europa.eu/trade/policy/in-focus/ceta/index_en.htm> accessed 22 July 2017

European Commission, 'Factsheet on Public Procurement in TTIP' (14 July 2016) <http://trade.ec.europa.eu/doclib/docs/2015/january/tradoc_153000.3%20Public%20Procurement.pdf> accessed 12 June 2018

European Commission, 'Will EU firms be able to bid for public contracts in Canada?' <http://ec.europa.eu/trade/policy/in-focus/ceta/ceta-explained/index_en.htm#public-contracts> accessed 22 July 2018

European Commission, Trade, *Joint Report on the EU-Canada Scoping Exercise* (5 March 2009), http://trade.ec.europa.eu/doclib/docs/2009/march/tradoc_142470.pdf accessed 6 July 2018

European Commission, *Communication from the Commission to the European Parliament, the Council, the European Economic and Social Committee and the Committee of the Regions, Making Public Procurement work in and for Europe*, Strasbourg, (3 October 2017) https://eur-lex.europa.eu/legal-content/EN/TXT/?uri=COM%3A2017%3A572%3AFIN accessed 15 July 2018

European Commission, CETA, 'Summary of the final negotiating results' <http://trade.ec.europa.eu/doclib/docs/2014/december/tradoc_152982.pdf> accessed 21 July 2018

European Commission, 'Guide to the EU-Ukraine Deep and Comprehensive Free Trade Area' <https://eeas.europa.eu/sites/eeas/files/tradoc_150981.pdf> accessed 7 May 2018

European Commission, Trade Policy, *Turkey Policies, Information and Services*, <http://ec.europa.eu/trade/policy/countries-and-regions/countries/turkey/> accessed 11 June 2018

European Commission, *Study of the EU-Turkey Bilateral Preferential Trade Framework, Including the Customs Union, and an Assessment of Its Possible Enhancement* (Final Report, 26 October 2016) <http://trade.ec.europa.eu/doclib/docs/2017/january/tradoc_155240.pdf> accessed 12 June 2018

Delegation of the European Union, Application for accession of the United Kingdom to the Agreement on Government Procurement in its own right, (1 June 2018), <https://docs.wto.org/dol2fe/Pages/FE_Search/FE_S_S009-DP.aspx?Language=E&CatalogueIdList=245666,245668,245669,245670,245671,245719,245701,245667,245658,245655&CurrentCatalogueIdIndex=5&FullTextHash=371857150> accessed 21 July 2018

Department for International Trade, *Trade White Paper: Preparing for our future UK trade policy, Government Response*, (January 2018), <https://assets.publishing.service.gov.uk/government/uploads/system/uploads/

attachment_data/file/671953/Trade_White_Paper_response_FINAL.pdf> accessed 28 May 2018

European Commission, 'DG Internal Market, Industry, Entrepreneurship and SMEs, Economic efficiency and legal effectiveness of review and remedies procedures for public contracts', (April 2015) <https://publications. europa.eu/en/publication-detail/-/publication/e07de115-c72a-4bd8-9844-daed732da34f> accessed 22 July 2018

EFTA, 'The European Free Trade Association' <http://www.efta.int/eea/eea-agreement> accessed 11 June 2018

European Union Delegation to Australia, 'Inquiry into the Commonwealth Procurement Framework Submission 3', Canberra, 24 March 2017 http:// www.aph.gov.au/DocumentStore.ashx?id=759dc14f-835b-42bd-a11e-a2c2e349eca8&subId=509292 accessed 15 July 2018

Green, D, Opinion, 'Blue passports and public procurement, Why Brexit may mean more public contracts going to foreign companies', *Financial Times* <https://www.ft.com/content/7fcd730e-2ddd-11e8-9b4b-bc4b9f08f381> accessed 30 March 2018

Getting the Deal Through, 'Public Procurement: Switzerland', (July 2017) <https://gettingthedealthrough.com/area/33/jurisdiction/29/public-procurement-switzerland/> accessed 6 July 2018

Global Affairs Canada, 'Canada-European Union Joint Report: Towards a Comprehensive Economic Agreemen't <http://www.international.gc.ca/ trade-agreements-accords-commerciaux/agr-acc/eu-ue/can-eu-report-can-ue-rapport.aspx?lang=eng> accessed 22 July 2017

House of Commons Research briefing, *The European Economic Area,* (House of Commons Library, Number 8129, June 6 2018) <https://researchbriefings. parliament.uk/ResearchBriefing/Summary/CBP-8129> accessed 11 June 2018

Home Office, 'Statement on passport contract', 22 March 2018, <https:// homeofficemedia.blog.gov.uk/2018/03/22/home-office-statement-on-passport-contract/> accessed 22 July 2018

HM Government, *Response to EU Commission's position paper of 7 February 2018, Article X Implementation Period*, (Explanatory Note 2018) <https:// assets.bwbx.io/documents/users/iqjWHBFdfxIU/rQVCUXtdp4QM/v0> accessed 10 June 2018

HM Government, *Other Separation Issues- Phase2,* (Technical note, March 2018), <https://assets.publishing.service.gov.uk/government/uploads/system/ uploads/attachment_data/file/685748/Other_Separation_Issues_Technical_ note_March_2018.pdf>accessed 12 May 2018

HM Government, *The Future Relationship between the United Kingdom and the European Union*, (July 2018) <https://assets.publishing.service.gov.uk/ government/uploads/system/uploads/attachment_data/file/725288/The_ future_relationship_between_the_United_Kingdom_and_the_European_ Union.pdf> accessed 16 July 2018

OJEU Contract Notice, 2017/S 058-107947, 23.3.17, Passport Production and Associated Services <http://ted.europa.eu/TED/notice/udl?uri=TED: NOTICE:107947-2017:TEXT:EN:HTML&src=0> accessed 15 July 2018

Organisation for Economic Co-operation and Development, 'Government at a Glance' (*OECD Statistics*, 2017) <http://stats.oecd.org/Index.aspx?QueryId=78406> accessed 3 June 2018

Negotiators Of The European Union And The United Kingdom Government, *Joint Report On Progress During Phase 1 Of Negotiations Under Article 50 TEU On The United Kingdom's Orderly Withdrawal From The European Union*, (8 December 2017) <https://www.gov.uk/government/uploads/system/uploads/attachment_data/file/665869/Joint_report_on_progress_during_phase_1_of_negotiations_under_Article_50_TEU_on_the_United_Kingdom_s_orderly_withdrawal_from_the_European_Union.pdf> accessed 10 June 2017

Negotiators of the European Union and the United Kingdom Government, 'Joint Statement on progress of negotiations under Article 50 TEU on the United Kingdom's orderly withdrawal from the European Union', (19 June 2018) <https://ec.europa.eu/commission/sites/beta-political/files/joint_statement.pdf> accessed 24 June 2018

Practice Direction 51N – Shorter and Flexible Trials Pilot Schemes <https://www.justice.gov.uk/courts/procedure-rules/civil/rules/part51/practice-direction-51n-shorter-and-flexible-trials-pilot-schemes> accessed 24 June 2019

Report from the Commission to the European Parliament and the Council 'On the effectiveness of Directive 89/665/EEC and Directive 92/13/EEC, as modified by Directive 2007/66/EC, concerning review procedures in the area of public procurement', (24.1.17) http://eur-lex.europa.eu/legal-content/EN/TXT/?uri=COM:2017:28:FIN accessed 4 May 2018

Sommerlad, J, 'Brexit: Leavers in uproar over 'national humiliation' as blue passports contract 'handed to Franco-Dutch firm'', *The Independent* (22 March 2018) https://www.independent.co.uk/news/uk/politics/brexit-latest-blue-british-passports-contract-gemalto-national-humiliation-eu-exit-france-a8267761.html accessed 22 July 2018

Source acknowledgements and permissions

Index

Printed in the United States
by Baker & Taylor Publisher Services